Reading B1

Ten practice tests for the **Cambridge B1 Preliminary**

Michael Macdonald

PROSPERITY EDUCATION
www.prosperityeducation.net

Registered offices: Sherlock Close, Cambridge
CB3 0HP, United Kingdom

© Prosperity Education Ltd. 2022

First published 2022

Revised edition published 2023

ISBN: 978-1-913825-77-5

This publication is in copyright. Subject to statutory exception and to the provisions of relevant collective licensing agreements, no reproduction of any part may take place without the written permission of Prosperity Education.

'Cambridge B1 Preliminary' and 'PET' are brands belonging to The Chancellor, Masters and Scholars of the University of Cambridge and are not associated with Prosperity Education or its products.

The moral rights of the author have been asserted in accordance with the Copyright, Designs and Patents Act 1988.

For further information and resources, visit: www.prosperityeducation.net

To infinity and beyond.

Contents

Introduction	2
About the B1 Preliminary Reading	3
Test 1	**5**
Test 2	**17**
Test 3	**29**
Test 4	**41**
Test 5	**53**
Test 6	**65**
Test 7	**77**
Test 8	**89**
Test 9	**101**
Test 10	**113**
Answers	**125**

Introduction

Welcome to this edition of sample tests for the Cambridge B1 Preliminary Reading, which has been written to replicate the Cambridge exam experience and has undergone rigorous expert and peer review.

This book contains 10 Reading tests (Parts 1–6), comprising a total of 320 individual assessments.

You or your students, if you are a teacher, will hopefully enjoy the wide range of texts and benefit from the repetitive practice, something that is key to preparing for this part of the B1 Preliminary (PET) examination.

I hope that you will find this resource a useful study aid, and I wish you all the best in preparing for the exam.

Michael Macdonald
Madrid, 2022

Michael Macdonald is a teacher, ELT writer and blogger. He has helped to prepare thousands of Cambridge candidates for exams. He is the Director of Prosperity English Language Academy.

About the B1 Preliminary Reading

The B1 Preliminary English language exam is the third of six levels established in the Common European Framework of Reference (CEFR): A1–C2. Candidates of all ages can take the B1 Preliminary test. In this book we have provided content with topics applicable to all age groups, including adult learners.

In the exam you will have 45 minutes to complete the Reading paper. This section has six parts, and is worth 25% of the final score.

Candidates will need to:

- answer multiple-choice questions to show understanding of short messages, as well as longer texts.
- match people to the correct service, holiday, experience, etc. that they are looking for.
- complete a text in which sentences have been removed by choosing the correct sentence.
- complete gap-fill tasks with, and also without, multiple-choice options.

The notices and texts should be similar to those found in real-world settings. Candidates must demonstrate their ability to understand and operate in such environments by choosing the correct answer. They will be asked to show command of vocabulary and grammar, as well as understanding of how a text is structured. Candidates must understand details, general meaning, as well as the writers' attitudes and opinions.

At the end of the examination, candidates will be given five minutes to copy their answers into the write-in answer sheets.

For more information, visit the Cambridge Assessment English website.

Prosperity Education

Our growing range of tests cover the IELTS Academic and Cambridge English B1 Preliminary (previously known as the PET), B2 First (FCE), C1 Advanced (CAE) and C2 Proficiency (CPE) **exam.** They are available in print or as pdfs which you can download directly from www.prosperityeducation.net. Each resource has a free **sample** so that you can evaluate its quality.

    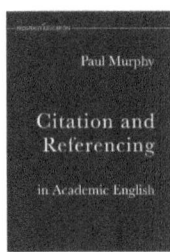

Cambridge B1 Preliminary Reading

Test 1

Cambridge B1 Preliminary Reading

Part 1

Questions 1–5

For each question, choose the correct answer.

1

Children must not be left unattended in the play area at any time during their visit

A Adults are not permitted in the children's play area.

B Children must always be accompanied by an adult.

C Children must stay to the left in the play area.

2

Hi Tim, Isa called for you earlier. I said you'd be in after 4pm. Remember you need to pick up that letter from the post office. You need to take your ID and sign for it. Angus

Delivered

Angus is telling Tim to:

A collect something from the post office.

B call Isa.

C get some new ID.

3

Dear Customers,
Store capacity is now reduced.

Please queue to the left.

A Do not try to buy so many things.

B The number of people permitted in the shop is less than it was previously.

C Only enter after someone has left.

4

Loyalty card available. Buy 10 hot drinks and we will give you another free of charge the next time you visit.

A Buy ten hot drinks, get one free next time.

B Buy nine hot drinks, get one free today.

C Buy ten drinks and get a loyalty card.

5

To all employees,
Because of essential building work, the coffee room will be closed until further notice.

A The coffee room is only for workers.

B The coffee shop is closed today only.

C The coffee shop is closed indefinitely.

Cambridge B1 Preliminary Reading

Part 2

Questions 6–10

For each question, choose the correct answer.

The people below are all looking for a new place to live.
On the opposite page there are descriptions of eight potential homes.
Choose which home would be the most suitable for the people below.

6  Stuart has just finished university and is looking for a room in a cheap, relaxed shared house. He doesn't have a car so he needs to be close to public transport links.

7  Mary Anne is an architect who is looking for something quiet in a rural area with lots of space. She would like to work from home sometimes. She is looking for a home which will accommodate her two pet dogs.

8  Colin is a student and wants to share with one other person who is tidy and responsible. He needs something with parking for his car. He would like his girlfriend to come to visit at the weekend sometimes.

9  Lin needs an apartment for the next three months. She wants to live alone. She would like somewhere close to the centre of town, and would like something which she doesn't have to decorate.

10  Trish needs a house for her husband and two young children, and her dog Rover. She needs parking for two cars, and would prefer to be close to a nursery school and primary school. She needs somewhere for just after the summer, as they will be on holiday in August.

Accommodation Available

A A four-bedroom, semi-detached house with a garage and extra parking is available from September. Large garden. Pets welcome. Easy access to the motorway and town centre. Close to several outstanding schools.

B A shared house with four students who like to party. The room is inexpensive and situated in Dobberton, just ten miles from Cambridge. You'll need a car, but we have lots of space for parking.

C Fully furnished luxury flat available for short-term lease. One bedroom, shower and bath, elevator and underground parking. All the modern conveniences. Owners prefer a single person.

D Room available in a flat with one other person. The room is spacious and airy, and inexpensive for its location, a two-minute walk from a bus stop and five minutes from the train station.

E A detached four-bedroom home is available near the old St Andrew's school site, located on the edge of town. Good access to all parts of town using the motorway. A family preferred. No pets though.

F A country cottage surrounded by tranquil countryside. Two bedrooms and one studio for home-working or study. Large garden. Pets welcome. Pre-installed security system and a good internet connection.

G Double room available in a small house with off-street parking. To share with studious 3rd year uni student who is often away at the weekend.

H Attic-type apartment available in the city centre. Large, quiet, open-plan space. Located just beside Coldham's park. Minimum 12-month contract.

Cambridge B1 Preliminary Reading

Part 3

Questions 11–15

For each question, choose the correct answer.

Violinist Alaina Masters talks about her job

I have always worked hard at mastering my instrument. That goes without saying. But ever since entering music college I was aware of how important it is to network with people. Since then, I've never really looked back and I am very happy to say that I've always managed to keep working.

When it comes to finding work, people who work for themselves, like me, must have various ways of making an income. I always need to be looking for jobs, or gigs, as musicians call temporary pieces of work. Those might come from orchestras or with smaller groups, such as the string quartet and jazz trio I usually play with.

I used to teach from time to time, but because I need to be available when a job comes up, I can't commit to having students anymore. It's a shame because I really enjoyed it.

The work with orchestras is always in the metropolitan area, which is handy for me. When I have one of those gigs, we will rehearse during the day in the weeks before the show starts. Those sessions are hard work and very tiring, but there is a social element to them and that helps get us through. Then we'll do a performance every night for the duration of the show, two on a weekend with some productions. That is always exciting and it's when I am in my element. The performances make all the effort worthwhile.

With my string quartet we play at weddings or other events, and that sometimes involves travelling. I don't drive, but thankfully one of the others is usually able to give me a ride, and we travel together for the concert. We try to always come back to our own beds afterwards, as paying for accommodation would use almost all our profits from the show.

Playing an instrument as a hobby and doing it to earn a living are quite different though. Thankfully, I have always maintained the love of what I do, so really, I never feel like I'm working.

Test 1

11 Alaina says her experience at college taught her the importance of
   A   building up connections in the scene.
   B   being good at her instrument.
   C   continually working.
   D   managing her time.

12 How would you best describe Alaina's work status?
   A   Self-employed, with one main job.
   B   Self-employed, with a variety of jobs.
   C   An employee of an orchestra.
   D   Unemployed.

13 What does Alaina say about teaching?
   A   She is accustomed to teaching now.
   B   She does not have time to teach any more.
   C   She would like to teach in the future.
   D   She hates teaching.

14 What does Alaina enjoy most about working with the orchestra?
   A   The fact that the rehearsals and performances are close to where she lives.
   B   The rehearsals.
   C   Performing.
   D   Seeing friends.

15 Which option best summarises why Alaina likes to get home after gigs?

A	She can't drive and her driver insists on it.	B	She is unable to sleep in a different bed.
C	It is impossible to find somewhere to stay.	D	To save money.

Cambridge B1 Preliminary Reading

Part 4

Questions 16–20

For each question, choose the correct answer.

Five sentences have been removed from the text below.
For each question, choose the correct answer.
There are three extra sentences which you do not have to use.

The Streaming Phenomenon

Watching the latest movies and series on demand is undoubtedly the biggest change in entertainment in the 21st century. The emergence of services such as Netflix and Disney Plus have revolutionised the way we watch TV, and how the TV and cinema industry function forever. Music listening is following a similar model. **16** ____ Gideon McFluff explains.

When people started making movies, they sold their product directly through the cinema theatres. **17** ____ It formed a lucrative industry for everyone involved. Many became rich and famous. Millions more around the world also earned a living, such as the camera operators, the make-up artists or the ice cream sellers in the theatre. And so it continued for many years.

Piracy – copying movies or music and then selling them illegally to individuals to watch at home – became a problem in the 1980s and early 90s. **18** ____ Sites such as Napster offered users the option to share movies and music for free. People no longer had to pay for what they watched or listened to. Something had to be done.

As internet technology has become more powerful, the necessary means have arrived in our homes. Broadband and fibre optic capability has enabled us to receive images and audio in real time. **19** ____

With such developments, companies now offer a convenient and legal way to watch your favourite media productions. **20** ____ What distinguishes one from the other is the available content. These companies need the most popular movies and series to attract subscribers. We have seen the streaming companies become the financiers of movies and series, enabling media companies to invest in top-quality productions.

Test 1

A If you wanted to watch the latest release you went to the cinema theatre and paid for your ticket.

B Nowadays 4G and Wi-Fi allow us to watch movies even when we are on the move.

C But did this change occur by choice or necessity?

D This then becomes the content for the streamers' libraries, which therefore attracts subscribers.

E Police and legal services eliminated the problem.

F Clients pay a subscription fee every month for access.

G However, with the arrival of the internet and the digital format the issue changed from problematic to catastrophic.

H Where can you get your favourite music or movies?

Cambridge B1 Preliminary Reading

Part 5

Questions 21–26

For each question, choose the correct answer.

The Potato

Solanum tuberosum, otherwise known **(21)**_____ its common name, the potato, is the world's fourth largest food crop, **(22)**_____ rice, wheat and maize.

It was first cultivated by the Inca-native Americans in Peru somewhere around 8,000 BC to 5,000 B.C. Spanish Conquistadors took over Peru in 1536 and discovered the potato for themselves, and subsequently transported them **(23)**_____ Europe.

Introduced to Ireland in 1589 it **(24)**_____ nearly 40 years for the potato to spread to the rest of Europe. It then made its way back across the Atlantic, this time to the North American continent, this time taken by European immigrants to the New World.

Potatoes are easy to grow, contain most of the vitamins required, and provide a **(25)**_____ yield from the space they occupy than the other staple crops.

The potato became the first vegetable to be grown in space in 1995. The University of Wisconsin and NASA invented the technology aimed at cultivating food **(26)**_____ astronauts on long space voyages, and, in the future, feeding space colonies.

21	A	for	B	by	C	at	D	on
22	A	after	B	before	C	over	D	when
23	A	over	B	on	C	of	D	to
24	A	took	B	lasted	C	played	D	told
25	A	best	B	good	C	worst	D	higher
26	A	from	B	in	C	for	D	make

Part 6

Questions 27–32

For each question, write the correct answer.
Write **one** word for each gap.

Sleep

Few people doubt the importance of a good night's sleep. But **(27)**_____ much do you need? Some people famously claim **(28)**_____ need as little as three hours' sleep per night, while others need nine hours or more just to function properly.

A good way **(29)**_____ find out how much sleep you need is to find a time such **(30)**_____ an annual holiday when you can sleep as much as you like. Take a note of the time when you go to sleep and wake up every day for seven days. Write **(31)**_____ down and finally work out the average you need daily by dividing the total by 7.

To give **(32)**_____ an idea, people commonly need between six and eight hours' sleep per night. However, everyone is different. Try it and see how much time you need in bed.

Cambridge B1 Preliminary Reading

Test 2

Cambridge B1 Preliminary Reading

Part 1

Questions 1–5

For each question, choose the correct answer.

1. Smoking is only permitted in the designated areas

   A You are not allowed to smoke here.

   B You can only smoke in selected zones.

   C Stand here if you want to smoke.

2. DO NOT OPEN THE WINDOW WHILE THE VEHICLE IS MOVING UNDER ANY CIRCUMSTANCES

   A The window must not be opened for any reason while the train is moving.

   B Only open the train window if there is a good reason.

   C Do not open the window until asked to do so.

3. If the football match is cancelled because of the rain, we'll go to the cinema instead.
   Delivered

   A If it is raining, we can go to the cinema.

   B If the football match does not take place, we can go to the cinema.

   C The sender would prefer to go to the cinema instead of the football match.

4

Television Studio 1
When the red light is on, recording is in progress. Do not enter while the red light is on.

A Don't go into the studio if the red light is on.

B You can enter when the red light is on.

C Turn the red light on if you want to enter.

5

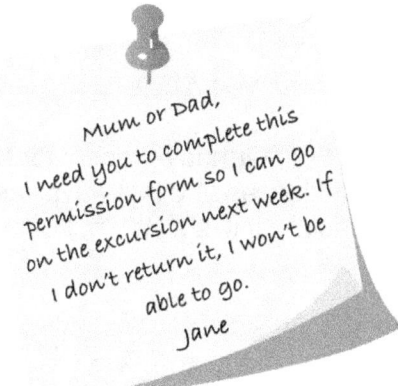

Mum or Dad,
I need you to complete this permission form so I can go on the excursion next week. If I don't return it, I won't be able to go.
Jane

A If Jane is not in school next week, she cannot go on the excursion.

B If Jane does not get a document signed by a parent, she cannot go on the excursion.

C If Jane wants her mum or dad to come on the excursion, they need to notify the school.

Cambridge B1 Preliminary Reading

Part 2

Questions 6–10

For each question, choose the correct answer.

The people below all want to have a day out in the south of England.
On the opposite page there are descriptions of eight days out.
Choose which day out would be the most suitable for the people below.

6  Hamid has two daughters, aged 5 and 6. They all enjoy swimming, and love nothing more than a good splash around in a pool. Hamid likes to sit and read the newspaper with a good cup of coffee!

7  Pankaj is looking for a 50th birthday present for his wife. She loves exciting experiences and is always keen to try something new – especially if it is a little out of the ordinary.

8  Maria lives in the middle of London and just wants to get away from the city for a while. She feels her 6-year-old daughter Lois spends far too much time indoors and should be able to enjoy herself in nature – and maybe even climb a few trees.

9  Horace and his wife Sandra are looking for a fun day out with their grandchildren. They enjoy dressing up, dancing and a bit of nostalgia. Horace thinks his grandchildren spend too much time playing computer games and should see what life was like before technology became so popular.

10  Ibrahim is a fan of motor sports and has been watching Formula One since he was a small child. He enjoys driving and wishes he could experience life as a racing driver for real.

Days Out in the South of England

A Up, up, and away!

Bernard's Balloons offer hot-air balloon tours every weekday from May to September. Be prepared to set off at 7am to enjoy the early-morning views over our glorious local countryside. Our chef-prepared packed breakfast is a great way to start your three-to-four-hour journey.

B Satisfy your need for speed with a visit to one of the top racetracks in the UK for an unforgettable experience driving one of our supercars. After a quick but thorough safety briefing, it will be time to take the wheel and enjoy a three-mile top-speed tour of the track!

C A Day at the Races

Join the crowds at one of England's most prestigious horse racing meets. VIP tickets available for those who would like to get close to the horses and riders.

D 1960s Day at Horsham Museum

Our annual 1960s Day, this year on June 15th, is always popular with families of all ages. A variety of stalls offer a real insight into life in the 1960s, from children's toys and games to army training. The restaurant offers authentic meals (including the always-popular fish and chips), and the energetic can try their hand at rock 'n' roll dancing.

E Weedly Water Garden is an exclusive spa, suitable for anyone who just wants to relax and enjoy a luxurious rest. Why not take one of our excellent beauty or massage packages? We have several pools, saunas, and a steam room and a gourmet restaurant for lunch or dinner.

F Wallington Water World is a brand-new swimming and water splash park with a variety of pools, rides and slides. Inflatable rafts and other toys are available for the adventurous, while younger children can enjoy a fun splash in Timmy's Toddler Pool. Our new cafeteria serves snacks and hot drinks for the grownups.

G Visit Grumble's Forest for a fun day in the woods, suitable for all ages. Pony-rides, tree climbing, rope ladders and woodland adventure playgrounds are just some of the fun activities for the adventurous. An ideal antidote to life in the city.

H Loop Hill games arcade is completely full of video games old and new. This is perfect for a rainy day as all of the activities are inside. Visit the exhibition which takes you through the history of video gaming. In addition, there are demonstrations and the chance to try some of the best new games on the market.

Cambridge B1 Preliminary Reading

Part 3

Questions 11–15

For each question, choose the correct answer.

Susan talks about life with her therapy dog, Benjy

I've been working with children for most of my life – I was a teacher and then a teaching assistant until I retired, but after a while I got bored and I was looking for a new way to get back to helping my community. My introduction to a local charity, Dogs in Schools, opened up a whole new chapter in my life. I volunteered to help, adopted a puppy and, four years later, here I am!

It's important to understand the difference between service dogs and therapy dogs. Service dogs, such as guide dogs for the blind or visually impaired, are highly trained and skilled animals that enable people to live their lives with confidence and security. Meanwhile, therapy dogs are used in schools, old people's homes and other locations in the community.

Benjy, my dog, spends a lot of time as a reading friend for primary-aged children in local schools. We've found the children love having someone to read to, and Benjy loves spending time with kids. He must know all of the Harry Potter books by now! We have relationships with 15 schools in the local area, and visit each of them once a month.

People often ask about what training Benjy has had. The answer is 'very little', but he has been carefully assessed by professionals to make sure he has the right temperament to work in the community. They look for calm, quiet dogs who enjoy the company of people and can deal with crowds or the unexpected without over-reacting. We also have to be very careful with Benjy's diet. He has to eat only dried food, as wet food contains bacteria that could be passed on to the people he is helping.

If you are interested in working with therapy dogs, I'd recommend contacting a reputable charity or organisation to make sure you're getting the very best training and understand all the needs of the dogs and the community before you begin. Plus, of course, they can help with things like insurance, the legal side and making introductions to the schools.

11 Susan said she became involved with Dog in School because
    A she had recently retired.
    B she was bored of being a teacher.
    C she wanted to help people around her.
    D she was lonely.

12 The text tells us in paragraph 2 that
    A service dogs are more important than therapy dogs.
    B therapy dogs are more important than service dogs.
    C some service dogs are therapy dogs too.
    D service dogs are more highly trained than therapy dogs.

13 Susan says Benjy loves
    A reading to the kids.
    B being with the kids.
    C hearing the children reading to him.
    D visiting 15 schools per month.

14 When selecting a therapy dog Susan says the most important thing is
    A the dog's training.
    B the dog's diet.
    C the dog's temperament.
    D the type of dog.

15 Which organisation would Susan recommend contacting to find out more about getting involved with therapy dogs?

| A | An insurance company. | B | A training company. |
| C | A local school. | D | A charity. |

Cambridge B1 Preliminary Reading

Part 4

Questions 16–20

Five sentences have been removed from the text below.
For each question, choose the correct answer.
There are three extra sentences which you do not have to use.

Spider-Man

One of Marvel Comics' most popular and long-lasting superheroes had an unlikely origin. **16** ☐ Lee hit upon the idea of a teenage superhero who would appeal to the young readers of his comics, with storylines that reflected their own lives. Spider-Man's home life, schooldays and relationship problems are just as important in the stories as his crime fighting. **17** ☐ So much so that Spider-Man got his own comic almost immediately.

As with many superheroes, there have been different versions of how Spider-Man got his powers, but they all tell the same basic story: high school science genius Peter Parker is bitten by a radioactive spider and wakes up with incredible strength and agility. He first tries to use his powers to make money as a wrestler. **18** ☐

The artist Steve Ditko, who created the iconic red and blue suit, is often neglected in the history of Spider-Man. **19** ☐ But he also invented the web shooters and helped develop many of Spider-Man's enemies.

There have been many different versions of Spider-Man. The original *Spider-Man Peter Parker* has been popular since the 1960s. **20** ☐ But an alternative version of Spider-Man, a young Hispanic New Yorker by the name of Miles Morales, is almost as popular in the comics and also starred in a hugely successful animated movie. There is also a time-travelling Spider-Man from the future, a Spider-Ham (a superhero pig) and a spider robot from Japan.

The huge success of the live action and animated movies of the past ten years proves that Spider-Man is one of the world's most well-known fictional creations.

Test 2

A But the story doesn't end there.

B However, when his guardian Uncle Ben is shot by a thief, he turns to crime-fighting.

C Peter has had several female love interests over the years, among them Gwen Stacy and Mary Jane Watson.

D Perhaps his key achievement was the hero's mask, which was designed to hide Peter Parker's young face.

E Spider-Man was created by the legendary writer Stan Lee in 1962 as a way to fill some space in an empty comic.

F The first publication was a fantastic success.

G His archenemy, The Green Goblin, did not appear until later.

H Peter has appeared in several movies, TV series, and video games.

Part 5

Questions 21–26

For each question, choose the correct answer.

M.O.T.D

Match of the Day, **(21)**_____ shows highlights of matches from the English football league, is the world's longest-running football-related television programme. It was first shown on 22nd August 1964. The show was broadcast in black and white and attracted an **(22)**_____ of around 20,000 viewers.

The show is now broadcast **(23)**_____ a Saturday night, and features highlights of all the games played which have been played that day. In recent years *Match of the Day 2* has joined BBC Channel 1 broadcasts to **(24)**_____ matches played on a Sunday. Both programmes typically draw millions of viewers, and as a result the BBC have introduced several related programmes on TV, radio and **(25)**_____ digital platforms.

In 2010 the show's theme tune was voted the most recognisable of all TV shows. Its team of presenters are all famous names, perhaps more because of appearing on the show **(26)**_____ because of their professional football careers which went before.

21	A	that	B	who	C	which	D	when
22	A	audience	B	assembly	C	army	D	onlookers
23	A	with	B	in	C	on	D	at
24	A	show	B	demonstrate	C	display	D	view
25	A	his	B	our	C	its	D	her
26	A	so	B	that	C	as	D	than

Part 6

Questions 27–32

For each question, write the correct answer.
Write **one** word for each gap.

The Next Superfood

Algae **(27)**_____ a versatile, nutrient-dense food which many have suggested as the superfood of the future. There are various different types of edible algae, such **(28)**_____ the blue-green variety, which includes spirulina, the brown variety, which you might find as kelp or kombu wakame, as well as the green and red variety.

Many types of edible algae contain high amounts of vitamins and minerals, including iron, folate, magnesium **(29)**_____ zinc. Spirulina and chlorella **(30)**_____ a very high protein content and lots of calcium can be found in kelp.

In addition to the health benefits, algae farming could be used to counteract global warming. It is easy to grow and it doesn't require a lot of resources to produce **(31)**_____. When farmed, it **(32)**_____ improve water quality due to its filtering effect, and it is very good at absorbing carbon dioxide.

Source: https://news.algaeworld.org/2020/03/an-introduction-to-algae-the-latest-superfood/

Cambridge B1 Preliminary Reading

Test 3

Cambridge B1 Preliminary Reading

Part 1

Questions 1–5

For each question, choose the correct answer.

1

Peter,
can you pick up the dry-cleaning on your way home tonight? I need my dress for my job interview next week.
Janet

A Peter needs to choose which dress Janet will wear to the interview.

B Peter needs to collect some clothes for Janet.

C Peter has to clean Janet's dress for her.

2

To: All Parents
Subject: Home Clothes Day

Dear Parents,
Next Wednesday is Home Clothes Day. Students must bring in a one euro donation if they do not want to wear their school uniform.

A Pupils have the option not to wear uniform next Wednesday.

B Pupils do not have to come to school next Wednesday.

C Pupils have to pay one euro to wear their school uniform next Wednesday.

3

Oh no, I forgot to feed the cat before I left the house this morning! Do you mind popping in to give him his breakfast?
Thanks!

Delivered

A Please go to feed the cat.

B Go to my house to have your breakfast.

C Did you remember to feed the cat?

4

Hi, could you see if Jake can come to the department store in town later?
He needs to try on and pick some new shirts and trousers.

Delivered

A Jake needs some new clothes.

B There is a sale at the department store.

C Jake needs to pick someone up from town.

5

Please note that all students must return their library books by next Thursday.
Any late books will result in a fine.

A It is OK to change your book next Thursday.

B Pupils' results for exams will be posted in the library next Thursday.

C Students must bring back the books they have borrowed by next Thursday at the latest.

Cambridge B1 Preliminary Reading

Part 2

Questions 6–10

For each question, choose the correct answer.

The people below are looking to adopt a dog from a pet sanctuary.
On the opposite page there are descriptions of eight dogs that are available for adoption.
Choose the best option for each person or people.

6  Iqbal works from home and has two children aged 8 and 12. He is looking for a dog who will give them all an excuse to do some daily exercise.

7  Shamim has just bought her first house with a garden. She doesn't have any pets at the moment, and can't wait to adopt her first dog to make the most of the space.

8  Marco and his wife love driving to the beach for long walks along the seashore. They're looking for a dog that will enjoy splashing around in the sea.

9  Ana already lives with two older dogs, and is looking for a younger dog who will add a bit of fun and energy to the house, without annoying them too much.

10  Jennifer is an experienced dog owner who has previously adopted dogs who have needed lots of support and care. She has plenty of time to spend with the dog as she has recently retired. A younger, male dog would be ideal.

Adopting a Dog

A Teddy is a small two-year-old dog who would need a female owner as he does not trust men. He has been in a number of homes that have not worked out, so we're looking for somebody with a lot of patience and understanding to take care of him.

B Benjy is very friendly and loves to be around other dogs that he can play with, so a home with other pets is ideal. He gets on well with dogs of all ages and seems to understand when they don't want to play.

C Rocky is a very cheerful and bouncy large dog looking for a home with active owners. If possible, they should enjoy playing ball games as he loves toys. He travels well in a car so would enjoy going for long walks away from home.

D Pickle is a friendly dog who would be suitable for a large home with a roomy garden for lots of exercise. He does not get on well with cats or other animals.

E Jack is an elderly dog who has a number of health conditions that require a lot of nursing and a special diet. He can only take short walks now and needs plenty of rest during the day. We're looking for someone with experience of caring for sick animals.

F Brandy is a very shy and retiring dog who ideally needs to be placed in a caring home who can also adopt his best friend Marley. When he's alone, Brandy tends to get very sad, but Marley makes sure he stays cheerful.

G Mindy is not comfortable around other dogs and will need to be kept on a lead when in public, so it is important that she has an owner who has had dogs in the past. She will need to be the only pet in the home.

H Sidney is a friendly dog who would like his new family to be at home with him most of the time, as he hates being left on his own. He gets on well with older children. As a young dog he needs to be walked twice a day if possible.

Cambridge B1 Preliminary Reading

Part 3

Questions 11–15

For each question, choose the correct answer.

Ravinder talks about his career as a paramedic

As a teenager, one of my favourite TV shows was a documentary about ambulance crews, and I knew almost immediately that I wanted to be a paramedic when I left school. My mum was a nurse, so you might think that's what made me want to work in the medical profession. But I think the TV show made it look more exciting.

As a paramedic you work in a range of emergency situations. You're often the first to arrive at the scene of an accident, and you have to quickly assess the patient's condition and select the correct treatment. You have to work alongside the police, the fire service, the friends and relatives of your patient and passers-by – so there are plenty of distractions! You have a variety of high-tech equipment at your disposal, so you need to be comfortable with technology as well as people.

My training took four years. It was a full-time course and a mix of lessons and practical work. They make sure you get to spend time with the ambulance service during your course, so that you get a taste for the life of a paramedic. That means you see the best and worst of the job before you begin.

To be honest the academic qualifications are only part of the job. Obviously, as a paramedic you come face-to-face with unpredictable situations almost every day. You have to be able to remain calm and keep your head. That's probably the most important skill we need to have, as you're often dealing with stressed, panicking or injured people. You have to stay focused, and communicate calmly and clearly to all of the people around you.

After a few years of working with the ambulance service, I was ready for a new challenge. I had a few different options. One was to continue with the ambulance service and become a team leader, but I didn't feel ready for that. I don't really see myself as a manager. Another option was to take a desk job and work as a telephone adviser from our control room, but that didn't really appeal to me either.

Fortunately for me, we have an air ambulance service flying from my hometown – the airport is only a few minutes from my house – and a job came up there. So now I'm a flying paramedic!

Test 3

11 Ravinder decided to become a paramedic
- **A** because his mother worked in a similar job.
- **B** because of an exciting television programme.
- **C** to drive quickly.
- **D** because school was finished.

12 When arriving at the scene of an accident the first thing to do is
- **A** speak to all the other emergency services.
- **B** get comfortable.
- **C** evaluate the patient.
- **D** deliver treatment.

13 Ravinder says the most important thing a paramedic needs to have is
- **A** the medical training.
- **B** the ability to keep calm under pressure.
- **C** a strong stomach.
- **D** a good knowledge of technology.

14 Why did Ravinder want to change jobs?
- **A** He hated working in an ambulance.
- **B** He wanted more responsibility.
- **C** He wanted something new to keep him interested.
- **D** He wanted to move house.

15 He took the job as a flying paramedic because

A	he couldn't get a job as a manager.	B	he always wanted to fly.
C	it was convenient from where he lived.	D	it was the most exciting option.

Cambridge B1 Preliminary Reading

Part 4

Questions 16–20

For each question, choose the correct answer.

Five sentences have been removed from the text below.
For each question, choose the correct answer.
There are three extra sentences which you do not have to use.

The Return of the Wolf

British people have become accustomed to seeing urban foxes eating from their rubbish bins, but for many the fox is the largest wild animal they will ever see. **16**

'Rewilding' is the philosophy that giving the countryside back to nature is one of the best ways of decreasing the decline in biodiversity in the world. **17** Perhaps most importantly, it has been calculated that rewilding could contribute significantly to reducing carbon emissions.

Wolves, along with lynx and beavers, have been called a 'keystone species' by the rewilding movement in the UK. It is believed that introducing these larger animals back into the British countryside will have a major impact on the rest of the environment. **18**

They force animals such as deer to move more often and over greater distances, which allows the plants that they eat to recover and grow back more strongly, and it also gives more space and opportunities to smaller animals, birds and insects.

Critics, however, say that too much importance is being given to the keystone species. They argue that reintroducing wolves could actually harm the progress being made by the rewilding movement. **19** But there is an obvious danger to livestock and even pets.

Rewilding is making significant progress. A key target for UK campaigners is the British royal family, which owns around 1.4% of British land, according to some sources. **20** The universities of Oxford and Cambridge and the Church of England are other major landowners that could significantly contribute to rewilding.

A Wolves and lynx, for example, help maintain the health of other animal species.

B However, the 'rewilding' movement has been going from strength to strength.

C There is only a very small chance of danger to humans.

D They have dismissed the idea.

E Not many would have seen a deer, and the bear is no longer native in the UK.

F It will also give animal and plant populations more of a chance to survive climate change.

G Representatives of rewilding organisations recently met with the team that manages the Royal Family's land.

H The pools created by beavers provide homes for fish and other wildlife.

Part 5

Questions 21–26

For each question, choose the correct answer.

Travelling by Train

It **(21)**_____ the train that first enabled people to travel easily over long distances. Some 200 years later the train is looking likely to be the public transport of the future.

In our current environmentally aware age, some progressive countries **(22)**_____ banned commercial national flights, investing instead in high-speed electric-powered trains. **(23)**_____ extensive rail networks already in place, the transformation of land travel is happening right now.

Modern trains in countries such **(24)**_____ Spain and Japan are punctual, spacious and comfortable. They are reasonably priced and have good access points, with stations in the city centre as opposed to airports **(25)**_____ are almost always a rail-journey away. Passengers have a generous baggage allowance and can generally arrive as little as ten minutes **(26)**_____ the train departs.

All in all, the road to the future might well be a track.

21	**A**	been	**B**	are	**C**	were	**D**	was
22	**A**	could	**B**	have	**C**	get	**D**	are
23	**A**	With	**B**	To	**C**	In	**D**	On
24	**A**	as	**B**	like	**C**	on	**D**	for
25	**A**	whose	**B**	which	**C**	who	**D**	than
26	**A**	under	**B**	apart	**C**	before	**D**	after

Part 6

Questions 27–32

For each question, write the correct answer.
Write **one** word for each gap.

Depression

The most common illness treated **(27)**_____ doctors in the UK is depression. **(28)**_____ is estimated that 10% of women and 5% of men in the nation suffer from clinical depression.

Depression costs the UK economy about £10 billion every year due to absence from work and **(29)**_____ cost of treatment. And it's not just a problem in the UK. Around 10% of Americans suffer from depression. Depression **(30)**_____ commonly diagnosed and treated in children nowadays too.

Exercise and diet, as with many illnesses, is the best treatment **(31)**_____ depression. However, as with many illnesses, those easy fixes are not always possible. So, many patients rely on antidepressant medication, which can give much needed support for those **(32)**_____ need it.

Cambridge B1 Preliminary Reading

Test 4

Cambridge B1 Preliminary Reading

Part 1

Questions 1–5

For each question, choose the correct answer.

1. Your parcel will be delivered between 1pm and 3pm today by your delivery person Jacques. You will be asked to sign to confirm delivery.
   Delivered

   A Your item will be delivered either at 1pm or at 3pm.

   B Jacques will call you to confirm the delivery time before he comes.

   C Your item will be delivered sometime during a two-hour period this afternoon.

2. You have just made a payment to the bank account ending 3456.

   If you think this is an error, please contact your bank immediately.
   Delivered

   A Please get in touch with your bank.

   B If this payment is not correct, get in touch with your bank.

   C There has been a mistake, so contact your bank.

3. HOSPITAL VISITORS

   Visiting hours are between 1 and 4pm.

   Please report to the reception desk when you arrive so that we can make a note of your contact details.

   A Please write down the visiting times.

   B Please leave your contact information at reception when you visit.

   C You must get permission from the reception desk to enter the hospital.

4

> Please log out of your computer at the end of your lesson so that the next class can begin straight away.

A To save time for the next class, please ensure that you have completely ended your session on the computer.

B Please leave the building immediately at the end of your class.

C Please switch the computer off when you have finished.

5

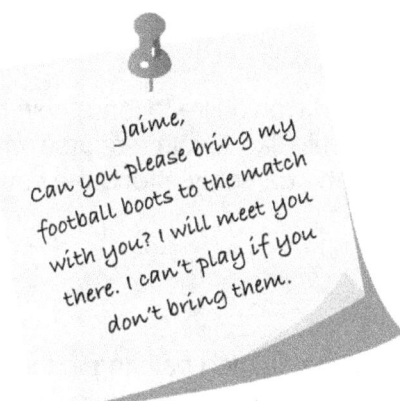

> Jaime,
> can you please bring my football boots to the match with you? I will meet you there. I can't play if you don't bring them.

A You can't play today.

B I need you to bring my boots so I can play.

C Please make sure you have the correct set of boots when you come to the match.

Cambridge B1 Preliminary Reading

Part 2

Questions 6–10

For each question, choose the correct answer.

The people below are all looking for a course to study.

On the opposite page there are descriptions of eight potential courses.

Choose which course would be the most suitable for the people below.

6  Mohammed is looking for a course on a weekend in which he can make something with his hands. He enjoys working with wood and would like to produce a present for his wife.

7  Sumitra loves clothes and would like to learn how to alter and repair them. She would like to join a course where she can meet new people. She can only attend the course one night per week.

8  Holly likes to paint and has studied painting in the past. She works until 7pm on Tuesdays and Thursdays.

9  Terry and Jill would like to learn a new activity together. They don't really mind what it is as long as they can get out of the house a couple of days a week during the morning and can do it together.

10  Scott is very interested in learning to make statues but has never tried it before. He is available from 6pm every weeknight, but works on weekends.

General Interest Courses

A Have you always wanted to learn to play chess? This club takes place on Tuesdays and Thursdays, from 10am–noon, in Regent's Park. Learn tactics and strategy like the GrandMaster. Bring a friend for a 10% discount on the monthly charge.

B Beginner's Art Class
Learn the basics of drawing, painting and sculpture. No previous experience necessary. Tuesdays and Fridays at the old Polytechnic.

C Carpentry for beginners
Come to learn to work with all natural materials. Make and decorate kitchen products of your own design. Wednesday evenings from September until May.

D Musical instrument making
Master luthier Damien Michaels will assist you in the manufacture of your own ukulele in this course. Previous experience of working with wood is preferable. Sign up for classes on Saturday mornings for September.

E Are you the fashion designer of the future? Learn to draw your own shoes, dresses and hats in this theoretical course on clothes design using traditional techniques and computer-aided design.

F Oil painting level 2
This intermediate-level course is the perfect continuation for those who studied on the beginner course last year or have previous experience. The class takes place every weeknight from 8pm.

G Upcycling is very popular at the moment. Learn useful skills for bringing old clothes back to life. This is one of our most popular courses, with a strong social element. Every Friday.

H Interior design is always popular, and on this course you can learn all the best tricks for turning your home into a modern palace. From 6pm Monday and Tuesday until December.

Cambridge B1 Preliminary Reading

Part 3

Questions 11–15

For each question, choose the correct answer.

Martin talks about his daily life as a dairy farmer

I've been a farmer all of my life. My grandfather bought this dairy farm and set up his first herd of cattle in the 1940s. My father grew up here, and so did I. There was no way I was ever going to escape being a farmer, even if I had wanted to! Luckily, I never even considered any other career.

I get up every day at around 6am, and I have to be out with the cows by 6.30am to start milking. It only takes around ten minutes to milk an individual cow, but it takes me a couple of hours to work through the entire herd. Once I've finished all of the milking, I have my breakfast and make sure the kids set off to go to school on time.

Mid-morning, the milk van arrives to take away the day's milk, and then I usually go to the office. You see, as well as the hands-on work, I also have to do all the paperwork and general business administration – doing the accounts, sending emails, phoning up suppliers and customers, and so on. That's my least favourite part of the job.

How I spend the rest of my day depends on the season. In the spring there are calves to check on, to make sure they're growing fit and strong. In the summertime, I often spend a lot of each day out in the fields, ploughing and cutting the grass for the cows to eat over the winter. And you can guarantee I'll spend at least some of my time each day mending machinery. Something goes wrong almost every day, so you can often find me fixing a tractor or working on something that has broken in the milking shed.

Obviously, when you work mostly outdoors, the weather can make life very difficult. Sometimes it rains every day for weeks and I'm completely covered with mud by around 8am. When it snows, I have to dig the snow off the roads so that the milk vans can come and go.

I always expected my life to be hard work, and I haven't been disappointed!

11 In the first paragraph Martin says
    A   he bought the farm when he was very young.
    B   his family have been on this farm for three generations.
    C   he wants to get a different job.
    D   he studied at university to become a farmer.

12 The first thing Martin does in the morning is
    A   send his children to school.
    B   eat his breakfast.
    C   milk some of his cows.
    D   milk all of his cows.

13 What part of his job does he not like so much?
    A   When he has to send the milk away.
    B   Administrative tasks.
    C   Using his hands.
    D   Looking after the animals.

14 What does Martin say about his daily routine?
    A   It changes because of the time of year.
    B   It is always the same.
    C   He spends less time fixing things than anything else.
    D   He has no way of knowing what will happen each day.

15 Overall, what does Martin say about farming?

A	It is too hard a job.	B	It is a difficult job, but as he expected it would be.
C	He would recommend becoming a farmer.	D	He would prefer not to have become a farmer.

Cambridge B1 Preliminary Reading

Part 4

Questions 16–20

For each question, choose the correct answer.

Five sentences have been removed from the text below.
For each question, choose the correct answer.
There are three extra sentences which you do not have to use.

Love in the Bin

In 2018 the art world was shocked by a daring stunt by the mysterious artist Banksy. The painting 'Girl with Balloon' sold for £860,000 at the Sotheby's Auction House in London. **16** ____ The moment the sale was completed, a beeping alarm started, and a shredder, hidden in the frame of the painting, began to destroy the image. Altogether, around three-quarters of the painting was cut into thin strips hanging underneath the frame.

A week later, Banksy uploaded a video which explained that the artist had actually planned to shred the entire painting. **17** ____ The video also showed the picture frame being put together with the shredder in Banksy's studio, and a photo from the auction house of somebody pressing the button that activated the shredding machine.

Sotheby's insisted that the auction house had not been involved directly in the stunt. **18** ____ They had had no reason to investigate any further.

After the shredding, there was more controversy. Banksy had claimed the original image was from 2006, but art experts claimed that the style of the image was more similar to his works from 2016. There were also claims that the artist had experimented with shredding art previously. **19** ____

The painting's buyer had no reason to regret their purchase. **20** ____ Sotheby's was keen to point out that this was a new, original artwork: "The point is, the work we are now selling is not the same work. This work was created on 5th October 2018 in the Sotheby's saleroom, and it has never been available for public sale."

Test 4

A Just two years later, in 2021, the partially shredded painting, now known as 'Love in the Bin', sold for an amazing £18.5 million.

B The video's caption said: 'In rehearsals, it worked every time.'

C Banksy's true identity is unknown and adds to the mystery.

D Imagine how you would feel if someone destroyed your newly purchased artwork.

E Then something shocking happened.

F However, Banksy said that the act of shredding the image during the auction was the real work of art.

G Before the sale, 'Love in the Bin' had been displayed in galleries in London, Hong Kong, Taipei and New York.

H They said that Banksy had insisted that the frame was an integral part of the artwork.

Part 5

Questions 21–26

For each question, choose the correct answer.

Slow Practice

The human body is capable of incredible things. **(21)**_____ look at a gymnast competing, a professional footballer controlling the ball, a magician performing a magic trick or a good musician playing a complicated piece of music. Some things appear to be so difficult that we assume the performers **(22)**_____ have some kind of super-human talent which we would never be able to match.

However, if you ask the people who know, the performers who we watch, and the teachers and coaches who have worked with them in **(23)**_____ career, they will tell you that the simple key is practice. And the right kind of practice: slow practice. If you can't do it slowly, you can't do it quickly. Simple, **(24)**_____ it?

Analyse what you are trying to do. Look at the mechanics of **(25)**_____ it can be achieved, and then work on it methodically. Technique is extremely important. Musicians practice scales, footballers do drills, magicians practice tricks in front **(26)**_____ the mirror hundreds of times. Slow down to make big steps forward.

21	A	Nearly	B	Only	C	Just	D	Hardly
22	A	must	B	should	C	will	D	had
23	A	a	B	whose	C	their	D	its
24	A	wasn't	B	isn't	C	doesn't	D	didn't
25	A	what	B	who	C	why	D	how
26	A	of	B	with	C	on	D	in

Part 6

Questions 27–32

For each question, write the correct answer.
Write **one** word for each gap.

Elephants

The elephant is the largest **(27)**_____ all land animals. An average male stands around three metres tall and weighs six tonnes. Even an elephant baby, which is called a calf, is huge, weighing around 120kg. Those baby elephants **(28)**_____ stand up within 20 minutes of being born. They live for 60–70 years.

Elephants are native to Africa and Asia. The African species is bigger in general and **(29)**_____ larger ears in comparison to its body. The African elephant appears to have two 'fingers' **(30)**_____ the end of its trunk, whereas the Asia elephant has only one.

Famously, elephants **(31)**_____ forget. They can make long journeys during migration, remembering water holes. In captivity they have been noted to recognise other elephants and humans they have **(32)**_____ seen for many years.

Cambridge B1 Preliminary Reading

Test 5

Cambridge B1 Preliminary Reading

Part 1

Questions 1–5

For each question, choose the correct answer.

1

Mr Smart is sick today.

Please complete the task set on your Google Classroom for today.

A Write to Mr Smart on Google Classroom.

B Do the work left by Mr Smart.

C Mr Smart will be late for class.

2

NO ENTRY!
EXCEPT WHEN
ACCOMPANIED BY
AUTHORISED
PERSONNEL

A Never enter this area.

B Don't enter this area unless you have a good reason.

C Only enter this area with a person who has permission.

3

Mum,
can you wash my red uniform for school please? We have PE on Wednesday and if I don't wear the red one I can't do it.
Jemima

A The red uniform must be worn on days when Jemima has PE.

B Jemima must not wear red on Wednesday.

C Jemima does not want to do PE.

4

Sarah,
I can't make it to the theatre tonight because of work. Do you want to offer my ticket to someone else?
Mike

Delivered

A   The show at the theatre is cancelled.

B   Sarah can give Mike's ticket to someone who can use it.

C   Mike wants to take someone else to the theatre.

5

To: you@youremail.com
Subject: Unable to process payment

We could not complete payment for your monthly subscription to A1 TV. Please update your payment details.

A   There was a problem, and we were not able to take money from your account.

B   Please check your bank before the next payment date.

C   Your payment is complete.

Cambridge B1 Preliminary Reading

Part 2

Questions 6–10

For each question, choose the correct answer.

The people below are looking at attraction parks for a day out.

On the opposite page there are descriptions of eight parks which are available. Choose the best option for each group.

6  Jessica and her family love rides which involve water. They will arrive by car so need parking. They would like to have accommodation as part of a family ticket. All the family like to have a wide choice of food.

7  Mollie and her kids love animation movies and would love to meet some of their favourite characters. The children are 8 and 5 years old, and she would prefer somewhere that caters for that age range. The children love making things and being entertained.

8  Maria and her two friends want to go on big, exciting rides. They don't drive so need good transport links. They are students and are looking for offers to save a bit of money.

9  Billy's family love animals and would love to see some during the day. They are all very sporty and would also find a place where they can do activities too. None of the family eat meat, but like eating in restaurants.

10  Mark and his family love all things related to cowboys. They would like to watch a show and go on some water rides which are good for all the family. They will be travelling by public transport so need good links to the city centre.

Attraction Parks

A   Dizzy World

The magical world of kids is waiting for you. Meet the most famous cartoon friends from all your favourite movies. This park, specifically for our younger visitors, has a variety of rides, as well as workshops in painting and a show with circus clowns.

B   High Towers

Come to ride The Screamer, the fastest roller coaster in the world, as well as 15 other fast and furious rides. Enjoy discounted tickets by visiting between Monday and Friday. Well-connected by train and bus.

C   Aqua World

Located 15 miles from the nearest city, this park is a world of its own. We offer overnight packages for all the family. Tickets include meals at the all-you-can eat World Buffet restaurant. Public transport to this park is limited but it does have free parking with all tickets.

D   Cowboy Country

See a Wild West cowboy shoot-out and a wonderful horse-riding show. Ride the white-water rapids and the Rocky Mountains roller coaster. Suitable for all ages. You will need your own transport.

E   West and Wet

This Wild West-themed adventure park is perfect for all the family. Learn to ride horses, and watch Wild Bill Hickup performing in the mid-day extravaganza before journeying into the White Water World. All rides are child-friendly. Well-connected to London by train.

F   West Farm World

A wonderful day out for all ages at our interactive farm. Horse riding, feeding the pigs, rides on the tractor, and much more. Get the real feel of a working farm. You will find an amazing mix of animals from around the world, including emus, buffalos and penguins. Later on, come to our award-winning restaurant for the best fresh meat in the country.

G   New Bridge Fountains

This wonderful new development offers some of the best water rides in the country. Ride the big wheel, enjoy the underground aquarium and the luxury restaurant. It is more expensive than other attractions parks in the area but worth the extra cost. Unfortunately, the hotel will not open until next season.

H   Nature World

For lovers of the outdoors, this is a new-age theme park. You will arrive on our electric train which travels through the huge safari park. Wander around the tropical gardens and find out about exciting new innovations in conservation. There are several adventure playgrounds, water sports and rock-climbing activities. Visit Vegan Village for excellent plant-based food.

Part 3

Questions 11–15

For each question, choose the correct answer.

Dev talks about how he transformed his parents' restaurant business

My father and mother got their start in the restaurant business when they were very young, and by the time I was born they had the best-respected Indian restaurant in our area of London. To be honest I wasn't that interested – although I was always glad to earn a bit of extra money by helping out when I was a teenager! But I was always more focused on building my own career.

By the time I was 30, I had built up a successful small company myself, but in 2017 I made a few bad investments and I lost the business. However, I like to think that I'm very resilient, so I picked myself up and began looking for a new opportunity.

I was inspired by a visit to my grandparents who live near Mumbai in India. I noticed that at lunchtime the streets filled up with guys on bicycles and mopeds, loaded up with dozens of little tin containers. It turned out that they were delivering prepared hot meals to all of the local businesses. When I got home, I took one look around my local area and noticed all the office workers coming out at lunchtime to buy boring sandwiches and generic salads from the local mini supermarkets.

I knew that curry is Britain's favourite meal (chicken tikka masala – roasted chunks of chicken served in a coconut and tomato sauce – is a particular speciality). Surely, I thought, people might enjoy a choice of Indian dishes at lunchtime? Especially if it was delivered straight to their desk!

Luckily for me, I had a well-known Indian restaurant at my fingertips! It took a while to persuade my father to get involved, but eventually my mother and I experimented by visiting a lot of local offices at lunchtime. After a couple of weeks, word got around, and people began to get in touch to ask if we would visit their buildings. My father was convinced.

A few years later, I have been able to take on some extra staff to deliver the food in my local area. I'm working on a plan to set up a national network of restaurants.

Test 5

11 In the first paragraph Dev says that when he was younger
    A   he always wanted to become part of the family business and help it grow.
    B   he was very interested in the family business.
    C   he always wanted to go to university.
    D   he was already more interested in his own business ventures.

12 How did Dev react to losing his business in 2017?
    A   He kept trying and looked for a new business idea.
    B   He suffered a lot and was very depressed.
    C   He got a job working for his parents.
    D   He moved to India.

13 Dev was inspired to start his delivery business
    A   after seeing a similar activity in Mumbai.
    B   when he saw how poor the choice of food was in Britain.
    C   after realising how popular curries are in Britain.
    D   because of all of the reasons above.

14 Dev's father accepted the idea because
    A   Dev's mother told him to.
    B   he realised there was a demand from the local offices.
    C   Dev's words convinced him.
    D   other companies were doing the same.

15 How would you describe Dev's plans for the future?

| A | He is still not very interested in the restaurant business, and he has other different plans of his own. | B | He is expanding the food-preparation and delivery business. |
| C | He is happy to continue what he is doing. | D | He has an offer to franchise his business. |

Cambridge B1 Preliminary Reading

Part 4

Questions 16–20

For each question, choose the correct answer.

Five sentences have been removed from the text below.
For each question, choose the correct answer.
There are three extra sentences which you do not have to use.

Bernard Palissy

In around 1540, Palissy saw a piece of fine pottery. **16** [ ] He became obsessed with the idea of recreating it for himself. For sixteen years he laboured in his workshop to create a copy. At times he even burned his furniture and floorboards to fuel his furnace.

Palissy never did find the secret of Chinese porcelain, but he did manage to invent a style of pottery all of his own. He added different metals and minerals, such as lead, iron and copper to his pots. That created bright, shiny colours. However, what made his pottery unique was his habit of adding drawings of animals and plants to the surface of his plates. **17** [ ]

In 1542 a French nobleman saw Palissy's pottery and was so impressed that he gave him the job of designing some houses and gardens on his estates. **18** [ ] His royal friendship proved useful in more ways than one. Palissy was a Protestant and offended many influential people with his views, but he escaped many punishments. It is thought that the Queen's help saved him from the St Bartholomew's Day Massacre, in which between 5,000 and 30,000 people died.

Palissy's influence went far beyond pottery and design. During his years in Paris, he set up a series of lectures in natural science. He spoke about volcanoes, earthquakes and the transport of water. His opinion was that science was useless unless it was based on direct observation and experimentation. **19** [ ]

Palissy's observations of wildlife and his experience of taking moulds from animals and plants led him to challenge ideas about fossils. Some people thought that fossils were leftovers from the Great Flood. However, Palissy argued that a 40-day flood would not bury animals as deeply as fossils. By looking at recently deceased sea urchins, he worked out that the mysterious 'fairy loaves' were fossilised urchins without their spines. He realised that another fossil represented a species that had died out at some past time.

At the end of his life, Palissy's religious beliefs eventually got him into trouble. **20** [ ] To the end he refused to take back some of his more controversial statements.

A   This philosophy underpins modern scientific method.

B   He instead suggested that fossils could be much, much older.

C   By 1548 he was in Paris, designing gardens for the Queen of France.

D   The item was possibly Chinese porcelain.

E   Palissy was born around 1510 somewhere in France.

F   His observations of animals were also important.

G   Aged 80, he died in the Parisian prison the Bastille in 1590.

H   The creatures were often moulded from real specimens collected from the marshes near his home.

Cambridge B1 Preliminary Reading

Part 5

Questions 21–26

For each question, choose the correct answer.

Major Tim Peake – Astronaut

(21)_____ you ever wanted to travel really far away? Tim Peake did exactly that when he travelled all the way into outer space, after spending six months on the International Space Station (ISS). During his stay he also walked in space, the first British person ever to **(22)**_____ so.

Tim was born **(23)**_____ the 7th April 1972, the son of a midwife and a journalist. As a young boy, his father would often take him to air shows. There he developed a love of aeroplanes and a fascination with flying.

By 16 he had decided to become a pilot in the army. Tim **(24)**_____ an officer, a pilot and a helicopter instructor. After more than 20 years, during which he accumulated more than 3,000 flying hours, Tim retired from the army.

He successfully applied to join the European Space Agency (ESA) and train to become an astronaut. Three years later he **(25)**_____ assigned a mission to the ISS. However, it took two further years of training and preparation to be ready for the mission.

During the Principia Mission Tim took **(26)**_____ in more than 250 scientific experiments. About 1.6 million schoolchildren in Europe engaged with the ESA's outreach program of at least 30 projects during his time in space. He famously ran the London marathon on a treadmill on the ISS.

21	**A** Have	**B** Did	**C** Can	**D** Are
22	**A** feel	**B** do	**C** make	**D** see
23	**A** for	**B** in	**C** at	**D** on
24	**A** became	**B** because	**C** began	**D** between
25	**A** were	**B** was	**C** will	**D** would
26	**A** place	**B** part	**C** over	**D** note

Part 6

Questions 27–32

For each question, write the correct answer.
Write **one** word for each gap.

New play park opens this week

The local council is pleased to announce the opening **(27)**_____ The Happy Kids Play Area in North Park on Friday this week. This new development features roundabouts, swings and **(28)**_____ 80-metre zip slide, among other attractions.

The space **(29)**_____ open from 9:30am every day until 8pm in the summer and 5pm in the winter. The area is supervised by a park attendant. However, children **(30)**_____ the age of 10 should be accompanied by an adult.

Every Saturday and Sunday, **(31)**_____ April to September, science workshops will take place at 10am, with teachers from Comberton Community College leading the session. You **(32)**_____ sign up for these sessions at www.northpark.com/sciencetime.

Cambridge B1 Preliminary Reading

Test 6

Cambridge B1 Preliminary Reading

Part 1

Questions 1–5

For each question, choose the correct answer.

1

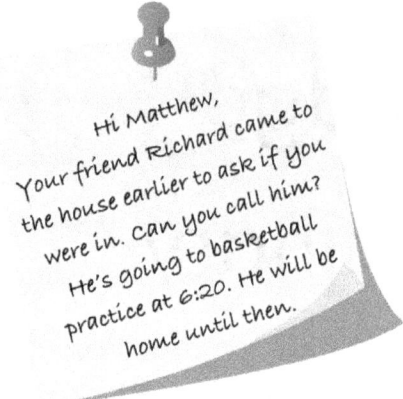

Hi Matthew,
Your friend Richard came to the house earlier to ask if you were in. Can you call him? He's going to basketball practice at 6:20. He will be home until then.

A Call Richard before 6:20 tonight.

B Call Richard after 6:20 tonight.

C Go to Richard's house to see him.

2

Please remove your shoes before entering the temple.

Worshipers are asked to please be aware of other people and keep noise to a minimum at all times.

A Please swap shoes before entering the temple.

B Please be as quiet as possible.

C Ensure you have the right shoes when you leave the temple.

3

After-school football club starts again on Friday. Those interested in attending should go to see Matt at morning break to register today or Thursday. You will need to get a permission form signed by a parent.

A If you want to go to football club, you need permission from parents.

B Football club will take place at break time today and Thursday.

C Matt will decide who can go to the football club.

Test 6

4

Evan,
Donna's party starts at 7 tonight. I will come by your house on the way there, around 6.30, and we can go together. Make sure you are ready.
David

Delivered

A   Evan should meet David at the party.

B   Donna will meet David at the party.

C   David will go to Evan's before the party.

5

To: All staff
Subject: Science lab windows

To all teaching staff:
Please ensure that the windows to the science lab are left open at the end of the day for ventilation. The cleaners will close them before they leave school.

A   The windows should be left open all night.

B   The windows should be left open after class.

C   Make sure you close the windows.

Part 2

Questions 6–10

For each question, choose the correct answer.

The people below are planning to go to the cinema.
On the opposite page there are descriptions of eight movies currently showing.
Choose which one would be best for each viewer or group.

6  Pretti and Omar want to see something fun with the kids this weekend. They would love to watch a movie and then be able to have lunch afterwards. The whole family loves musicals

7  Lee would like to take his girlfriend Katie to see a fun movie. Katie is a music teacher, so Lee would like something with good songs in it. Katie is away on a trip this weekend, so it needs to be during the week.

8 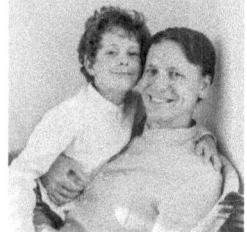 Tom wants to take his son to see a movie. Liam, his son, likes grown-up themes but is still only 12. He has said he wants to see something with lots of action but suspense too.

9  Yvette wants something to take her mind off her job as a doctor. She loves comedies, but doesn't like animations. She really enjoys travelling and seeing interesting wildlife and landscapes.

10  Sharon and Nadia are university students, and want to go to see a serious film which will stimulate them and make them think. They love movies with powerful female characters

A Day at the Cinema

A James Bonde is a British spy who needs to use his brain as much as his muscles in this latest instalment of the saga. The movie features some great fight choreography and several edge-of-your-seat car-chase scenes, and develops into a fine psychological thriller by the end. Parental guidance.

B The new Pixar animation premiers this week, and we have a special screening on Thursday evening only. Milly is a street cat who gets lost and needs to find her way home. Wonderful songs sung by singers you will recognise which are guaranteed to be big hits. Great fun for all ages.

C Police investigators are called to a small town when a local school teacher goes missing. Anthony Hoopkiss stars in this suspense/thriller, which is definitely for an adult audience only. Cath Winless is sensational as the smart female detective who will need all her skills to solve this mystery.

D David Attenburger's latest documentary film brings the natural world to life on your screen. A thought-invoking look at life in some of the most remote areas of the world, and how they are being affected by global warming. A great instrumental soundtrack by composer James Pickering accompanies the images.

E Country Folks tells the story of two brothers from rural Alaska who come to the big city. The feel-good script is very funny in places and the story has a beautiful moral. Director Ishmael Kalinder manages to include breath-taking images of the countryside to highlight the differences between the two environments.

F Kids' club this Saturday and Sunday morning features Snow White, the Disney classic. This original version has the same appeal it has always had, and there will be a special sing-along at 11am before the screening to teach the audience all the favourite songs.

G Doggie-style is a hilarious movie by Ken Tong, telling the story of Kenny and Kev, two poodles who just love to party. These animated friends make lots of adult jokes, and will make you laugh so much you might need a doctor.

H Meet Your Maker is an all-action movie in which tough leading-man Geffory Pleck plays Harry Smith. A gangster tries to take money from local businesses, but messes with the wrong man when he walks into Harry's hardware store. Strong language and scenes of violence from the start.

Part 3

Questions 11–15

For each question, choose the correct answer.

Alessandro Ricci talks about his unique job

Whenever I go to a party or meet new people, there is one question I hate: "What do you do for a living?" I can almost guarantee that they will laugh. Then, when I tell them that I needed a university degree and several years' training in order to get my job, they often don't believe me.

It's true that Ice-cream Taster sounds like any kid's perfect job. But ice-cream is a big business. As Chief Taster for one of the biggest ice-cream companies, I am responsible for developing new flavours. Those new products are essential for keeping us in the number one position.

Obviously, my most important talent is my sense of taste. I have to follow a few simple rules in order to keep it in good condition. First, however tired I feel in the morning, I must never drink coffee. Instead, I have to drink tea, or even better, herbal tea with no caffeine. Second, I have to avoid spicy foods such as curry which can hide more delicate flavours. And obviously, I must never smoke.

But I also have a secret weapon: a golden spoon. Again, people laugh when I tell them this, but gold is the ideal material because it leaves no aftertaste. This is very important when tasting.

I don't get to eat my products. Instead, I taste ice cream like a wine taster. I take a small bite, move it around my mouth, and then spit into a bowl. I make notes about the flavours and then move on to the next sample. I might try 60 different mixtures a day, so it's important to use a consistent vocabulary when I am describing them.

And after all of that, do I even enjoy ice cream? The truth is that I can take it or leave it. My favourite food on a sunny day? Fish and chips.

11 How does Alessandro feel when people ask him about his job?

   A   Sad.
   B   Proud.
   C   Dishonest.
   D   Embarrassed.

12 In paragraph 2 what does Alessandro say about his job?

   A   A child could do it.
   B   It's important for maintaining his company's position.
   C   He deals with marketing.
   D   He just tastes the current flavours.

13 To maintain his excellent sense of taste, Alessandro must

   A   never drink coffee.
   B   avoid strong flavoured food.
   C   never smoke.
   D   do all of the above.

14 Why does Alessandro use a special spoon?

   A   It makes him feel like a winner.
   B   The material does not affect the taste.
   C   It's a kind of joke.
   D   To get the right amount of ice cream.

15 What does Alessandro say about tasting so much ice cream?

A	It makes him fat.	B	It makes him hate ice cream.
C	It makes him like wine.	D	He never swallows it.

Cambridge B1 Preliminary Reading

Part 4

Questions 16–20

For each question, choose the correct answer.

Five sentences have been removed from the text below.
For each question, choose the correct answer.
There are three extra sentences which you do not have to use.

Occupy Wall Street

In September 2011, a group of around 1,000 protestors met in Zuccotti Park in New York. **16** However, the police moved the protestors away and they ended up in the park, just a few streets away from Wall Street itself.

By then, a few years had passed since the financial crash of 2008, which had been caused by the banks. **17** In order to save the economy, the US government had rescued the banks using taxpayers' money. To the protestors, it seemed as though the banks had escaped without taking any responsibility for their actions.

As it got dark on the first night, they got ready to sleep in the park. **18** Therefore, they slept with only sleeping bags and blankets. The protestors stayed in the park for several weeks. However, in November, the city and the park's legal owner eventually cleared the park as the cost of cleaning and policing had become too high. The protest had been generally peaceful. **19** Around 200 people were arrested.

The slogan of the Occupy Wall Street protest was 'We are the 99%'. This aims to highlight the fact that the super-rich, who are only 1% of the population, hold most of the power in society. **20** In the US its influence is still felt in more recent campaigns such as Black Lives Matter, in protests against student loans, and calls for a fairer minimum wage.

A New York's mayor explained: "People have a right to protest, and we'll be happy to make sure they have locations to do it."

B Initially tents were not allowed.

C The protest was originally planned to take place on Wall Street, in the financial district of the city.

D Non-violent protest was the only way.

E Still, there were some clashes with the police as the campaigners were removed from the park

F Banks had been lending irresponsibly and many Americans found themselves in massive debt as a result.

G The protest inspired similar protests in 951 cities in 82 countries.

H Banks are now required to be more transparent.

Cambridge B1 Preliminary Reading

Part 5

Questions 21–26

For each question, choose the correct answer.

Pablo Picasso

Picasso is undoubtedly the most famous and most successful artist of the 20th century. He **(21)**_____ born in Malaga in Southern Spain on the 20th of October, 1881. His first word was 'piz', his attempt at 'lápiz', the Spanish word for pencil. He received lessons in art, figure drawing and oil painting from the age of 7. His father actually gave up painting as a result of witnessing the skills of a 13-year-old Pablo, saying that his son had already become a better artist **(22)**_____ him.

His exceptional talent is evident in very early works **(23)**_____ as *Plaster Male Torso* from 1893 or *Portrait of the Artist's Mother* from 1896. Those pieces, painted when he was 14 or 15 and 17 respectively, are in the Realism style. They show his outstanding talent and sometimes are used as evidence to defend Picasso from critics **(24)**_____ doubt his true genius when viewing his later works.

In 1895 the Picasso family moved to Barcelona where Pablo attended the School of Fine Arts. He passed through his 'Blue' period living between Barcelona and Paris. It was **(25)**_____ France in 1907 that Picasso met Georges Braque. The pair were a huge influence on **(26)**_____ other. But it was Pablo who painted *Les Demoiselles d'Avignon* that same year. The work is considered to be the first Cubist work.

21	A	be	B	is	C	was	D	had
22	A	that	B	than	C	as	D	who
23	A	like	B	such	C	made	D	called
24	A	when	B	whose	C	who	D	which
25	A	on	B	in	C	at	D	where
26	A	each	B	every	C	one	D	all

Part 6

Questions 27–32

For each question, write the correct answer.
Write **one** word for each gap.

Book Reviews

When you are at school, a standard exercise might be writing about a book you have recently read to summarise **(27)**_____ happened and inform the reader about the main characters.

The reviewer should say how successful the writer has **(28)**_____ in telling the story. **(29)**_____ you didn't enjoy the story, you can say why, and even recommend improvements to the author's work.

In school, book reviews are used **(30)**_____ get you writing and reflecting. They are also useful to check your understanding of what you have read. In real life, reviews featured **(31)**_____ TV, the internet or radio programmes, as well as in magazines and newspapers, can make or break a publication. They are an important promotional tool. Critics could be a writer's best friend **(32)**_____ their worst nightmare.

Cambridge B1 Preliminary Reading

Test 7

Cambridge B1 Preliminary Reading

Part 1

Questions 1–5

For each question, choose the correct answer.

1

Visitors must be at least 140cm tall to ride this waterslide.
1 mat per person.

A You must be shorter than 140cm to go on this attraction.

B You need your own mat to ride this attraction.

C Your height must be 140cm or more to go on this attraction.

2

Hi,
I have borrowed your charger. Sorry! I left mine at home. If you need it back urgently, I'm in room 56.
Cheers.

A I have your charger in room 56.

B Your charger is in my house.

C Can I borrow your charger?

3

Penny has just messaged to say she can't come to the concert with us. Do you know anyone who might want to come instead? Let me know.

Delivered

A Penny needs a ticket for tonight.

B Do you know someone who wants to come to the concert?

C Do you have an extra ticket for tonight?

4

Any bikes found here will be removed.
A penalty fee will be charged in order to get them returned.

A Please do not leave bikes in this area.

B You can leave your bike here.

C Bring your bike back to here.

5

Paul, we are here outside the cinema waiting for you. Did you forget? We have tickets for the 6pm show. We'll leave the ticket with your name on it at the box office.

Delivered

A We are going into the cinema. Join us inside.

B We will get a refund for your ticket.

C We are not going to the cinema anymore.

Cambridge B1 Preliminary Reading

Part 2

Questions 6–10

For each question, choose the correct answer.

The people below are all looking for a place to eat in Madrid.
On the opposite page there are descriptions of eight restaurants.
Decide which home would be the most suitable for the people below.

6  Pablo wants to go out after he finishes his late shift at work. He finishes at 22:00. He loves spicy food, and is vegan, so no meat or fish are allowed.

7  Marta really looks after her health and believes you are what you eat. She really likes fish and shellfish but not fried food. She would like to be able to walk to the restaurant from her flat in the city centre.

8  Stefano wants an interesting restaurant to impress a visiting colleague for work. Meat. Spanish Wine. It's a business lunch and the company is paying.

9  Jamie has a big appetite and as he is a student, he needs to find something which is not expensive. He likes American-style food and would like somewhere cool.

10  Pasha is vegetarian and loves salad and pasta. She is in Madrid on holiday and would like to eat at lunchtime and, if possible, she would like to enjoy the good weather as she eats.

Restaurants in Madrid

A Herbabuena serves healthy vegetarian and vegan food. Large portions and a great-value 'menu of the day', served from 12:00–17:00. Only open until 22:00, which is unusual for Madrid. Book to avoid disappointment.

B Zombie serves maybe the best burgers in town. The skater-style decoration is very stylish. 2-for-1 evening Monday and Wednesday until 8pm.

C Malacatin specialises in the traditional dish *cocido*, a type of meat stew with chickpeas, cabbage and a mixture of beef, chorizo and other Spanish meats. Expensive but very memorable. Open from 8pm.

D Maharaj – all of our dishes are vegan-based, and then you can choose if you would like us to add your favourite meat or fish, or just leave it meat-free. We can prepare your food to your liking with regards to spiciness. The kitchen is open from 13:00 until late.

E Inti de Oro. Specialist Peruvian gastronomy. Fresh, healthy foods. Try our excellent seafood in a mouth-watering ceviche. Very central location.

F El Botin is the oldest continuously functioning restaurant in the world. Try the excellent Spanish meats and seafood, and a large selection of wine. Not cheap, but definitely memorable.

G Ginger is a great Mediterranean restaurant and serves a wide range of quality dishes. Unfortunately the terrace is not open at the moment due to the roadworks outside.

H El Buscon serves traditional Spanish food at the lower end of the price scale. Try their incredible mixed grill which is easily enough for two people to share.

Part 3

Questions 11–15

For each question, choose the correct answer.

How To Be An Excellent Salesperson

David Chew, an experienced sales manager, explains how to build a successful career in sales.

Sales careers are a popular choice for young people, often offering a good salary, a strong team spirit, and a chance to travel. Here are some characteristics of a good salesperson.

Keeping a positive attitude is the most important skill that you will need as a salesperson. Not everybody is going to want what you're selling – in fact, most people won't. Maybe even worse, many of the people you approach simply won't respond to you at all. If you are rejected you need to be able to keep going, and treat every new opportunity as a potential success.

You need to believe in your product, but it's also important to really know what you are talking about. It is essential to get to know the features and benefits of the product, and be able to communicate these to your customer. Strong product knowledge will give you the confidence to answer any questions that come up.

You need to be able to build good relationships with your customers. Partly this is about getting to know them as individuals, but it can be much more effective to get to know what they do for a living and the problems that they face on a daily basis. Understand what the customer is telling you when expressing their needs. You have to be able to respond to those needs accurately. Everybody loves someone who solves their problems for them!

Finally, you need to act with integrity and honesty. You must never lie to win a sale. You must have the trust of your customers, your managers and your business. If you have that, everything else will work out.

11 The first paragraph says salespeople have the opportunity for

   A   office-based working.
   B   job security.
   C   good pay
   D   meeting interesting people.

12 What is the most important characteristic a salesperson must have?

   A   Good sales skills.
   B   The ability to respond to customers.
   C   A positive attitude.
   D   None of the above.

13 What will give you the ability to answer questions about your product?

   A   Self-confidence.
   B   Knowledge of the product.
   C   Belief in what you are selling.
   D   The way you dress.

14 David says the most important element in developing the relationship with your customer is

   A   understanding the problems they face in their workplace.
   B   knowing them personally.
   C   being able to do their job.
   D   language skills.

15 Which of these is most important overall when working in sales?

| A | How much you can sell. | B | Being truthful and reliable. |
| C | Your team. | D | Your profits. |

Cambridge B1 Preliminary Reading

Part 4

Questions 16–20

For each question, choose the correct answer.

Five sentences have been removed from the text below.
For each question, choose the correct answer.
There are three extra sentences which you do not have to use.

King James

LeBron James, also known as King James, is considered one of the best basketball players in the world, with a killer combination of height (he is six feet, eight inches tall), strength, ball skills and leaping.

James was born in Akron, Ohio in 1984 and had a difficult early life. **16** But he showed early promise on the basketball court, and a kind-hearted basketball coach offered to look after the boy so that he could concentrate on his schoolwork and his sports.

17 He led his team to three state titles and was named 'Mr Basketball'. In 2003 he decided to join the NBA (National Basketball Association) instead of going to university. **18** He played for seven years for the Cleveland Cavaliers, not too far from his hometown of Akron, but they never won a title, so in 2010 LeBron decided to look for a new team.

There was so much interest in where LeBron would move that the TV channel ESPN had an entire show about it called 'The Decision'. LeBron announced that he was going to join Florida team Miami Heat. At the time the decision was controversial, and many of his former friends and colleagues were very critical of his choice of team and of the way the announcement was handled by the ESPN producers. **19** Nonetheless, his time with the team was successful. In the next four years Miami Heat reached the championship four times and won twice.

But LeBron missed Cleveland and moved back to the Cavaliers in 2014. That year the team finally reached the championship and came close to victory – although they did not win until 2016. **20**

On top of his awards in the US, he has won gold medals in the Olympic Games in 2008 and 2012. James is undoubtedly one of the most successful players in the history of basketball.

A Next, LeBron moved to the LA Lakers for yet another appearance in the championship.

B The coach's instincts about LeBron were correct.

C His commercial earnings are as large as any other sports person in history.

D In primary school he enjoyed reading.

E He was the youngest player ever to be drafted to the NBA.

F For the next year James was probably one of the most unpopular players in the NBA.

G Starting his professional career without going to university was difficult.

H His father was an ex-convict and wasn't around very much as LeBron was growing up.

Cambridge B1 Preliminary Reading

Part 5

Questions 21–26

For each question, choose the correct answer.

Mobile phones in school

Message to parents of all students

Parents are **(21)**_____ that pupils are not permitted to use mobile phones in school. If you feel it is necessary for your child to bring a phone, the device must be switched **(22)**_____ and kept in their school bag. Phones must not be switched on until pupils have left the school grounds.

Smartphones can cause disruption **(23)**_____ class and distract pupils. They can also provide an unfair advantage in tests by providing access to the internet or notes. Mobile devices are also extremely expensive and the school will not **(24)**_____ any responsibility for loss or damage to phones which may happen in school.

Pupils found using a phone in school will have it confiscated. A parent will be required to come to school to collect the phone at a **(25)**_____ time.

We thank you for **(26)**_____ cooperation and understanding in this matter.

21	A	said	B	reminded	C	spoken	D	remember
22	A	off	B	out	C	over	D	in
23	A	in	B	at	C	on	D	or
24	A	get	B	go	C	take	D	bring
25	A	longer	B	later	C	sooner	D	after
26	A	its	B	their	C	our	D	your

Part 6

Questions 27–32

For each question, write the correct answer.
Write **one** word for each gap.

A Walk in the Park

Scientific research **(27)**_____ shown that a simple walk in your local park can dramatically increase your well-being. In a world where many more people are working on computers **(28)**_____ many doing so at home, making a point of getting out for some exercise really can make a difference.

Look **(29)**_____ your day and decide when you can have this important break. Try to do it at the same time every day if you can. You could take **(30)**_____ lunch or your morning coffee to the park. Sit and enjoy your surroundings: the fresh air and vibrant colours, the singing of the birds, the wind in the trees or **(31)**_____ sun on your skin.

All that fresh air will get your blood pumping and lead to **(32)**_____ increase in endorphins. That helps to alleviate stress and depression.

Cambridge B1 Preliminary Reading

Test 8

Cambridge B1 Preliminary Reading

Part 1

Questions 1–5

For each question, choose the correct answer.

1

To: Theatre group
Subject: Well done!

Well done to everyone for a great first show last night. You did really well. Only 4 more performances to go!
From Luke

A Tonight is the last night of the show.

B Congratulations on yesterday's show.

C Four days until the show starts.

2

Class 8M – English

Mr Kenny asks you to read chapters 1 and 2 of *Treasure Island*. Then answer the questions you find on Google Classroom in your notebooks. Mr Kenny hopes to be well enough to return tomorrow.

A Do the work set in class time. Answer questions in your notebook.

B Write the answers to the questions on Google Classroom.

C Do the work set as homework.

3

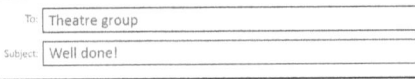

Please keep to the left when walking in the corridors. Stairwell 1 is for going up. Stairwell 2 and 3 are for coming down only.

A There is a one-way system in operation.

B Only walk on the right on stairs 2 and 3.

C You may walk anywhere on the left.

4

Charlie,
I won't be home until 7:30. Have a sandwich to keep you going until we get home. I'll cook when I arrive so you, dad and I can eat together.

A Don't eat until I get home.

B Eat something before I get home.

C Dad will make you food when he gets home.

5

Hi Liz, Have you seen my magazine? The one about guitars? I'm sure I left it in the living room, but it's not there now.
Gary

Delivered

A There was a magazine beside some guitars.

B Liz has read the magazine.

C Gary can't find his magazine.

Cambridge B1 Preliminary Reading

Part 2

Questions 6–10

For each question, choose the correct answer.

The people below are all surfing the internet.
On the opposite page there are descriptions of eight websites and online shops.
Choose the best option for each person.

6  René has just moved to a new city and would like to find out about some activities going on there. She is also keen to get to know some new people.

7  Tristan has just started a new job and would like to order some nice clothes for working in a law office. He does not have time to go shopping so wants to buy all the clothes online, but he needs to be sure that he can return them if he doesn't like them.

8  Alberto wants to find a really unusual gift for his girlfriend. He thinks she would like something creative and artistic that no one else has.

9  Charles would like to buy a guitar. He thinks that a used instrument would be more affordable for him, and if he can swap one of his guitars for another one, that would be even better.

10  Susan wants to buy a t-shirt for her son. He is a musician and likes anything music related. It is a birthday present, and she would like it sent directly.

Websites and online shops

A Sparks and Marks is a reliable seller that is renowned for its excellent no-questions-asked returns policy. High-quality clothes and furniture for professional people.

B Etsy is home to independent sellers of handmade goods. You will find something unique here. You can also commission artists to personalise or make items especially for you. For supporters of independent businesses.

C Musical Muster sells new instruments and accessories such as strings. You can also find any number of gifts for the musician – clothes, posters or whatever else you need – all packaged in our branded wrapping.

D Retro Online sells stylish second-hand clothes. From trousers to togas, this shop has everything for the fashion-conscious buyer. No returns are available unless the item is different to that advertised, but definitely some great bargains on this site.

E Ali Express has just about anything you need, with a wide range of prices and qualities. Many items do come from far away so read the delivery terms. Beware of import taxes as this can add on a significant amount to what you pay.

F Gum Tree is a marketplace for all sorts of items, but specialises in accommodation. Make sure to check out the reviews of users for your security and comfort.

G Reverb – Second-hand instruments sold by individuals. A wide-range available from all over the world. There is also the possibility of exchanging instruments with others. Look out for some really good deals here.

H Lingobongo is a great website for finding social activities and knowing what is going on in the city. You can also meet new friends on our social media platform.

Part 3

Questions 11–15

For each question, choose the correct answer.

Hedgehogs, the UK's Favourite Mammal

The hedgehog has been voted the UK's favourite mammal, winning more than 35% of the votes, but how much do most people know about these secretive creatures? Here are a few facts about how our spiky friends spend their year.

Winter

Hedgehogs hibernate all winter, and even if they wake up, they are not very active unless the weather is warm for the time of year. While they are sleeping they can lose up to a third of their body weight.

Spring

In March the hedgehogs begin to wake up. Unsurprisingly, they are very hungry and thirsty, so now is a good time to leave some hedgehog food out in the garden for them. As well as eating, they will be looking for a good place to build their nests. If you can, it's helpful to build piles of wood or buy a hedgehog house for them.

Early Summer

If you hear loud grunting at night, this could be hedgehogs mating. The females are pregnant for around four weeks, and usually give birth to six or seven baby 'hoglets'. After the birth, it is the mother's job to look for food for the children as they are too small to leave the nest for a while. The father is unfortunately no help, as he never visits!

Late Summer

During July the hoglets will be joining their mother as she hunts for food, although they still return to the nest for an occasional drink of milk. By August the young hedgehogs are large enough to go out into the world on their own. Hedgehogs are solitary creatures and so they may never see each other again.

Autumn

Food is becoming more scarce, so hedgehogs may need your help again. Leave out tinned dog or cat food. You can also buy special hedgehog food from some pet shops.

As it gets colder, hedgehogs will try to eat as much as they can to prepare for their winter hibernation. They will also begin to build their nests for the winter. By November, most of them will have settled down until next year.

11 In paragraph 1 we learn
    A   that there are many secrets about hedgehogs.
    B   about the hedgehog's habitat.
    C   that British people prefer hedgehogs to any other mammal.
    D   that 35% of British people have a pet hedgehog.

12 In winter hedgehogs
    A   migrate to a warmer climate.
    B   normally sleep all the time.
    C   are very hungry and thirsty.
    D   have babies.

13 In early summer
    A   you should build a nest for the hedgehogs.
    B   you might see some baby hedgehogs.
    C   the father hedgehog provides all the food.
    D   the babies stay in the nest.

14 Hedgehogs
    A   stay in groups as they grow older.
    B   all hunt as soon as they leave the nest.
    C   start to live alone.
    D   only grow spines if they are male.

15 The writer of the text

| A | recommends helping hedgehogs with appropriate food and building materials. | B | says that you can take a hedgehog into your home over winter. |
| C | suggests that hedgehogs are dangerous. | D | warns against doing anything to interfere with the animals' life. |

Part 4

Questions 16–20

For each question, choose the correct answer.

Five sentences have been removed from the text below.
For each question, choose the correct answer.
There are three extra sentences which you do not have to use.

The International Space Station

The American space agency NASA has announced that the International Space Station (ISS) will end its 32-year life in orbit in 2030.

The plan is that the space station will crash-land in the Pacific Ocean at a place known as Point Nemo. NASA says Point Nemo is 'pretty much the farthest place from any human civilization you can find'. **16** ____ It has become like a cemetery for space debris such as old satellites, because they are unlikely to hit human habitation as they fall.

The space station is shared by five different agencies: NASA, Roscomos (Russia), JAX (Japan), CSA (Canada) and ESA (Europe). **17** ____ It is used as a space laboratory for scientists in physics and astronomy, and for testing the equipment that will be used for possible manned space flights to Mars.

The space station's first component was launched in 1998. **18** ____ The station has been continuously occupied ever since, with crew members staying in orbit for up to six months. Life on the ISS is cramped and a little boring. **19** ____ This helps to avoid muscle loss. The food is tasteless, and the astronauts look forward to visiting spacecraft as a source of fresh vegetables. There is evidence that a prolonged stay in space has permanent effects on health, so becoming an astronaut is not a decision to be taken lightly.

The ISS consists of different modules, which were separately launched and assembled in space 400km above the surface of the Earth. This is considered a low-level orbit. The station travels fast. **20** ____ It is the largest artificial object in space and is visible to the naked eye as it orbits.

Test 8

A However, there were no astronauts on board until 2000.

B It travels around the Earth every 93 minutes at a speed of 7 kilometres per second.

C The savings will be used to fund research in deep space.

D It is 2,700km away from any human habitation.

E Altogether, 15 different countries have participated in the programme.

F It is likely that the future of scientific research in space will not be in NASA-owned space stations.

G Stress is common and astronauts must exercise for at least two hours a day.

H The journey to Mars will be all the more complicated.

Cambridge B1 Preliminary Reading

Part 5

Questions 21–26

For each question, choose the correct answer.

Hats

There are literally thousands of different types of hats. A hat is a shaped garment that is **(21)**_____ on the head. It can be made of any material which clothes can be made of.

Many hats indicate social status. A crown is a type of hat that proclaims royal birth. People have worn headdresses in all cultures throughout history **(22)**_____ religious and ceremonial purposes.

A chef's hat, for example, **(23)**_____ indicate rank and experience. In the military, peak caps and berets signify seniority or belonging to a particular group. Students wear a flat mortar board during **(24)**_____ graduation ceremonies.

Hats can also have a practical **(25)**_____. Workmen, soldiers, some sports people and people operating certain types of vehicles use hats for protection. **(26)**_____ the other hand, hats can be worn purely as decoration and are an important fashion accessory for both men and women.

21	A	shown	B	brought	C	worn	D	driven
22	A	for	B	of	C	in	D	at
23	A	have	B	are	C	can	D	must
24	A	my	B	their	C	its	D	our
25	A	thing	B	purpose	C	cause	D	play
26	A	On	B	In	C	Of	D	To

Part 6

Questions 27–32

For each question, write the correct answer.
Write **one** word for each gap.

Ukulele Club

This year's ukulele club is available to all Year 7 students on Tuesdays, **(27)**_____ lunchtime, starting on Tuesday, the 14th of September. Participants should eat their lunch and then come **(28)**_____ the music room to begin at 2:30pm.

If you do **(29)**_____ have your own ukulele yet, you can borrow one of the school's. Ukulele club is free and is open to everyone. You do not need **(30)**_____ previous experience of playing.

If you have your own instrument, you should **(31)**_____ it to the music room during morning reception and leave it in the secure cupboard at the back of the music room. Please make sure your name **(32)**_____ written clearly on the case.

Cambridge B1 Preliminary Reading

Test 9

Cambridge B1 Preliminary Reading

Part 1

Questions 1–5

For each question, choose the correct answer.

1

Class 7J

Go to the library for your 6th lesson. Answer the questions on pages 34 and 35 in your topic booklet. When you have finished you may read quietly.

Mr O'Reilly

A You should read for all of the 6th lesson.

B Read if you finish your first task.

C Read pages 34 and 35 of the topic booklet.

2

Hey Chris,
Are we still going to play snooker tonight? If so, we need to reserve a table before 6pm so let me know.
Graham

Delivered

A Chris and Graham are playing snooker at 6.

B Chris and Graham are going for dinner.

C Chris wants to confirm if he is meeting Graham to play snooker.

3

To: All staff
Subject: Tonight's meeting.

The link for tonight's meeting is below for any staff at home. Everyone else should attend in person in the assembly hall at 5pm.

https://meet.google.com/pfa-qvky-c

A The meeting is online for everyone.

B You can attend online if you are not in school.

C Every person must attend the meeting in the assembly hall.

4

Hi Suzanne,
Would it be possible to post this letter for me? It just needs to be stuck in the post box. There is one on your way to school.

A Post the letter if you can.

B Buy a stamp, stick it on the letter, and post it.

C Take this letter to school.

5

Calderglen Camping.

Please note:

No fires!

No music after 8pm.

A No fires after 8pm.

B No music allowed.

C Fires are not allowed.

Cambridge B1 Preliminary Reading

Part 2

Questions 6–10

For each question, choose the correct answer.

The people below are all looking for a new place to go for a holiday.
On the opposite page there are descriptions of eight destinations.
Choose the best one for the travellers.

6  Solange wants to take the family somewhere with a beach, but where she can see some famous sights too. Her son is crazy about football and her daughter loves animals.

7  Ibrahim is taking his new wife away for their first holiday and would like to take her somewhere romantic. They would like to see a museum or two, and eat well.

8  James and Carlos want to go to a resort with lots of other young people. They don't have a lot of money, but they still want to party and do as many activities as possible.

9  Jing and Felix would like to visit a city with a strong musical tradition. They want to enjoy sunshine and visit at least one cultural attraction. They prefer a smaller city.

10  Arun and Paulo want to visit a historical city, with a castle. They both love ghost stories and would like to see something spooky. They also love to see live performances of all kinds. They are both teachers so they want to go in the summer holidays.

European Holiday Breaks

A Bulgaria is the coolest new holiday destination. Sunny Beach on the Black Sea offers lots of experiences, such as beach sports and karting, as well as great nights out, and all at the most affordable prices in Europe.

B Visiting Scotland's capital Edinburgh is always a great experience. You will see street performers everywhere during the Festival in July and August. To see the castle make sure you book in advance. The Ghost Tour through the old city is a highlight.

C Madrid, the Spanish capital city, is full of things to do. Visit The Royal Palace, the Prado Museum and of course the football stadiums of Real *and* Atletico Madrid. Madrid is right in the centre of the country but has great rail links to the coast.

D Paris is often said to be the city of love. But while there you can also see The Eiffel Tower, The Mona Lisa at The Louvre and enjoy some of the best cuisine in the world.

E Amsterdam, with its many canals and museums, is full of wonderful attractions. Visit the Rijksmuseum, the flower market, or the house of Anne Frank. Hire a bike or ride the tram to get around.

F New York is one of the biggest and most exciting cities in the world. Visit the incredible skyscrapers, Central Park and other iconic tourist attractions. Warm in the summer and freezing in the winter. If you need to change your clothes, New York is the place to go shopping.

G Granada, a small city in Southern Spain, is packed with lively bars and restaurants. Live music is everywhere, and you will be treated to some of the best Flamenco in the world. You can also visit the historic sites with La Alhambra Palace as the main attraction. Be careful with the sun as it commonly reaches 40°C in the summer here.

H Barcelona is a metropolitan city, which sits right on the Mediterranean coast. Visit the world-famous zoo, the Sagrada Familia cathedral or the famous football team's stadium before heading to the beach or Olympic port.

Part 3

Questions 11–15

For each question, choose the correct answer.

A Career in Gaming

If your parents ever accuse you of wasting your time playing computer games, you might want to tell them how much money top gamers make! Esports, short for electronic sports, usually take the form of multiplayer video game competitions. You can play as an individual or as a team, with the most popular games generally taking the form of large battles in which teams compete in a virtual arena.

Although esports have been in existence almost since the start of computer gaming, they only really began to grow in the 2000s. Since then, esports have been getting more and more popular every year, largely thanks to YouTube and the live-streaming platform Twitch, which allows fans around the world to watch esports events live. The total audience for esports events has been estimated at 454 million people, being most popular in China and South Korea.

The result is that professional computer gamers can now earn almost unbelievable amounts of prize money. At the highest level, prizes can be worth millions of dollars.

In 2012 the website Esports Earnings reported that prizes totalled $14 million. By 2021 the total increased to $144 million, with $40 million given out at a single event, an annual championship for players of the online game Dota 2.

The top 20 gamers on the Esports Earnings list are players of Dota 2. But other games can be almost as lucrative. A player of the game Fortnite, which launched in 2018, earned $3 million in 2019. And Korean gamer 'Faker' has earned almost as much playing League of Legends, winning the championship in his first season. He is still regarded as one of the best players in the world.

Professional gamers are expected to behave well, with organisations such as the International Esports Federation (IESF) keeping an eye on players' behaviour. As with real sports, there are examples of both good and bad behaviour – for example, there have been accusations of players fixing the results of matches for profit.

Another concern is that players live very unhealthy lifestyles, playing games for long periods and sleeping during the day – contributing to poor physical and mental health. So maybe your parents are right after all!

11 Multiplayer video game competitions are played
    A only by individuals against other individuals.
    B only in teams against other teams.
    C by individuals and groups.
    D in large halls filled with computers and users.

12 In paragraph 2 we learn that
    A esports were most popular in the year 2000.
    B the main platforms to play on are YouTube and Twitch.
    C YouTube and Twitch have helped esports become more popular than ever.
    D esports have only existed since 2000.

13 The writer says players of which game win the most money?
    A League of Legends
    B Fortnight
    C Dota 2
    D Esports Earnings

14 The International Esports Federation (IESF)
    A monitors players' behaviour.
    B always behaves well.
    C monitors players' eyesight.
    D repairs broken things during matches.

15 The writer says excessive gaming can be dangerous because

| A | parents don't like it. | B | it can affect your health. |
| C | it can make you badly behaved. | D | it makes you aggressive. |

Cambridge B1 Preliminary Reading

Part 4

Questions 16–20

For each question, choose the correct answer.

Five sentences have been removed from the text below.
For each question, choose the correct answer.
There are three extra sentences which you do not have to use.

Sloths

Sloths live in the tropical rainforests of South and Central America. They look a little like monkeys, with round heads, almost-human faces, long arms and shaggy fur, but actually they are closely related to anteaters. ⌊16⌋ The two-toed sloths are bigger and spend a lot of their time hanging upside-down from trees, while the smaller three-toed sloths will often sit up in their trees.

⌊17⌋ They move through the trees at a speed of around 40 metres a day, which is less than half the length of a football pitch. Even at that slow pace they get tired. Sloths can spend between 15 and 20 hours a day sleeping.

It's possible that sloths actually became slower in order to escape predators – their movements are unlikely to attract the attention of other animals, especially as they tend to grow green algae on their fur. But don't think they are harmless. ⌊18⌋ They are strong enough to hang by one arm from a tree branch as soon as they are born.

Sloths eat leaves, twigs and buds from the trees. ⌊19⌋ Their slow lifestyle means that they can survive on much less food than you'd expect.

⌊20⌋ They seem to enjoy it too, often dropping into the water for a quick splash and using those long arms to swim along. The only other time they leave the trees is for their weekly trip to the toilet.

A   Sloths are famous for their slow speed, and it's not surprising.

B   There are many famous cartoon sloths, such as Barney and Steve.

C   There are two different types of sloth, with two toes and three toes, and six species.

D   The biggest threat to the different species is deforestation

E   One surprising fact about sloths is that they are comfortable in water – in fact, they are excellent swimmers.

F   A sloth in danger will fight fiercely with its sharp claws and powerful arms.

G   As the rainforests are cut down for mining, agriculture and other human activities, the sloths have less and less space to live.

H   As they don't have sharp front teeth, they use their very firm lips to tear away their food.

Cambridge B1 Preliminary Reading

Part 5

Questions 21–26

For each question, choose the correct answer.

The Most Dangerous Animal in the World

In the natural world **(21)**_____ are many dangerous animals and every year humans are killed as a result of coming into contact with them.

Hippos are the 3rd largest animals on the land. They are **(22)**_____ notoriously grumpy and kill around 3,000 humans every year in their native Africa.

The crocodile is the 2nd deadliest reptile, being responsible for the deaths of 1,000 people every year. However, snakes, which live on every continent except Antarctica, are the 3rd most dangerous animal **(23)**_____ the world, killing an estimated 50,000 people each year. The tiny mosquito transmits malaria. One million people die annually **(24)**_____ a result.

In fact, the Number 1 position for the deadliest animal in the world goes to human beings. Homicides account for around 750,000 deaths annually, and wars could account for an average of 1,000,000 deaths. However, it is probably our actions, such as pollution, **(25)**_____ cause the most deaths around the world.

You might **(26)**_____ surprised to know the notorious shark was responsible for only 11 deaths in 2021.

21	A	who	B	there	C	these	D	those
22	A	too	B	but	C	also	D	well
23	A	at	B	on	C	in	D	to
24	A	as	B	with	C	like	D	of
25	A	why	B	which	C	who	D	when
26	A	be	B	think	C	are	D	do

Part 6

Questions 27–32

For each question, write the correct answer.
Write **one** word for each gap.

Beatrix Potter

Helen Beatrix Potter was born **(27)**_____ the summer of 1866 in South Kensington, London. Beatrix, as everyone called her, and her brother Beltran kept many pets such as rabbits, mice and frogs, and they loved **(28)**_____ draw them. She was home-schooled, and had several teachers, including an art tutor.

She had a keen interest in nature and science, and spent many hours searching **(29)**_____ and collecting examples of plants and insects. She would then record them by drawing and painting them **(30)**_____ writing about what she observed, using a good scientific method.

However, when Beatrix grew **(31)**_____ and started trying to publish her work, she suffered discrimination, as many people would not take her work seriously **(32)**_____ she was a woman. It is a testament to her excellent work that her drawings of some fungi are still used to this day in the scientific community.

Cambridge B1 Preliminary Reading

Test 10

Cambridge B1 Preliminary Reading

Part 1

Questions 1–5

For each question, choose the correct answer.

1

For Sale
Almost-new woman's bike.
Lights and helmet included.
Available right away.
£30.00

The bike:

A can be received now.

B can be exchanged for lights and a helmet.

C has never been used.

2

Peter,
I have hurt my leg and can't go to football training tonight. But why don't you come around to my house for some dinner and we can watch the Man Utd match? Barry

Delivered

A Barry might see Peter at football training.

B Barry might see Peter at the Man United match.

C Barry might see Peter at his house

3

What can we do better?
What do you like? Please put your comments in the box.
Best regards,
The Kitchen Staff

A Tell us only if you liked something.

B Tell us how to improve.

C Reserve here for your next visit now.

4

To: All tutors
Subject: Permission for photos

Could tutors remind students that unless they have returned their authorisation form from their parents they will not be able to participate in any school photos this year? The deadline for submissions is tomorrow.
With many thanks,
Ruprect Fitzgibbon, Headmaster

A Only pupils with written permission can be in the photos.

B Photos will be taken tomorrow.

C Parents need to come to school to collect photos.

5

Sorry we missed you!
Post Service

We tried to deliver your package today. You should allow 24 hours before collecting it.
Please bring this notification and a form of identification.

A Your package will be available today.

B Your package will be available for 24 hours.

C You need to prove who you are when you collect your item.

Part 2

Questions 6–10

For each question, choose the correct answer.

The people below are all looking for a new book.
On the opposite page there are descriptions of eight publications.
Choose the best book for each person.

6  Philip wants to buy a book for his 4-year-old son, who loves cute animals. Philip thinks it would be a good idea to have some content to help his son learn to spell when he reads it.

7  Albert loves reading murder mystery books. He needs a new publication as he has read almost all of the older books available, especially the popular ones.

8  Ray wants to read a book about a real person's life. He loves sport, and would enjoy something which is not too serious.

9  Maxime is 14 and would love to read an inspiring biography about an interesting celebrity. She loves music and dance and previously enjoyed a book about a singer with a football player boyfriend. She wants good value for money.

10  9-year-old Steven is choosing a book for his own birthday present. He loves adventure stories and would like something he could read more than once. He likes series.

A New Book

A Mrs Muddle is the new character from writer A.T. Smart, last year's best-selling author. If you buy *Mrs Muddle's Murders*, this detective story will make you think and have you guessing who done it. Entertaining from start to end.

B *The Search for the Lost City* is a multi-story book where you choose what happens in the story. Therefore, it changes every time you read it. Gilbert Homes is back as the hero in the third instalment of this action-packed story.

C The story of how a boy from Glasgow became the most successful football manager of all time, Alex McFish's autobiography will have you laughing out loud. Not always suitable language for younger readers.

D *Silly Snakes and Ladders* is a lovely book for younger readers. You play as you read through the short stories about Simon and his six serpent friends. All good fun.

E In the book *Eye Billy*, which is written by her best friend, Sally Brown, you will find out how Billy Eyelash overcame adversity, first becoming successful as a dancer, before finally going on to become the most famous pop singer in the world. The eBook contains links to YouTube videos and exclusive mp3 downloads which is a real bonus.

F *Alphabet Animals* is a book filled with pictures of all a child's favourite animals. Readers learn the names of the animals and this helps them to learn the alphabet. Great for schools and home.

G This re-issue of the classic by legendary writer Ernest Swift is one of the best-selling books of all time. If you haven't read *Murder in Mind*, make sure you do. It's still a wonderful book, even 80 years after its original release.

H *The Book of Birthdays* is a manual for buying great presents, whoever they might be for. You'll find more than 200 original present ideas, making sure all the presents you give in the future will be memorable and unique.

Cambridge B1 Preliminary Reading

Part 3

Questions 11–15

For each question, choose the correct answer.

Could these apps be the next TikTok?

Social media platforms have a habit of disappearing. Few teenagers nowadays have even heard of MySpace, Vine or even Google Plus. It's possible that one day even TikTok will disappear. But, with more than three-billion downloads, the app seems to be going from strength to strength. It has, however, been damaged by nationwide bans in India, for example. In 2020, President Donald Trump also threatened to ban the Chinese-owned app in the US, but he failed to carry out his promise.

But if TikTok does vanish, where will we go next for silly dances, funny clips, cute pets and the latest music? Here are some apps you might like to think about using instead…

American company Clash offers the ability to upload 21-second looping videos, and might tempt video creators to join with the promise of small payments called 'DROPs' from their fans.

Dubsmash focuses on short, lip-synched videos. Users can access a big library of music to add some sound to their videos, but a unique feature is a library of famous movie quotes. Although nowhere near as big as TikTok, it still has more than 100 million downloads – not a bad start!

Funimate is a great platform for making videos with your friends, but has the downside that you have to pay to access some of its features.

The Cheez platform is all about comedy, fashion and vlogging. You can win rewards for uploading videos that get lots of likes – but also for liking a lot of videos yourself. Some popular activities on Cheez include dance battles and other competitions.

Similarly, the Chinese platform KWAI encourages competitions by regularly posting challenges for its users, meaning you can stay one step ahead of the latest viral trends. This is obviously a successful idea, because KWAI was used by an average of one billion people a month during 2021.

So, there are many alternatives to TikTok out there, but of course we recommend being careful with what you share. Please try to avoid sharing things you'll regret later, and make sure that you understand the age limits on all of these apps (for example, you shouldn't use TikTok if you are under 13).

11 In the first paragraph the writer tells us that social media platforms

　　A are always successful.

　　B are the enemy of governments.

　　C have come and gone quickly in the past

　　D are no longer popular.

12 Which app would allow users to look like they are singing their favourite songs?

　　A KWAI

　　B Dubsmash

　　C Cheez

　　D Funimate

13 Which app is successfully suggesting activities for users?

　　A KWAI

　　B Dubmash

　　C Cheez

　　D Funimate

14 Which app can earn you prizes based on your interaction?

　　A KWAI

　　B Dubmash

　　C Cheez

　　D Funimate

15 The main purpose of the article is

A	to warn about the dangers of social media apps.	B	to highlight improvements to some apps.
C	to inform us about new social media apps that might interest us.	D	to review some apps.

Part 4

Questions 16–20

For each question, choose the correct answer.

Five sentences have been removed from the text below.
For each question, choose the correct answer.
There are three extra sentences which you do not have to use.

Living as an artist

Sarah MacPee talks about life as an artist.

People often ask me how someone becomes an artist. **16** ☐ I spent about the first 20 years of my professional life working in marketing. I really enjoyed the creative element of marketing, such as the different ways you can represent and sell a company. In the end, I felt that I needed a change from the 9-to-5 and decided to embrace the artist's life. Up to now, it's a decision which has worked out very well.

I've always been artistic. **17** ☐ I was always painting and drawing pictures (my mum still has every painting I gave her when I was growing up). I didn't study Art at university, but I did study it at school until I was 18.

I'm always learning new skills. That might be on the internet, from TV, from friends or in workshops. **18** ☐ And I use all of these in my work.

On a typical day I start at my beautiful desk, situated in front of a big window. That inspires me. I get warmed up by doing a bit of drawing, sometimes painting. I generally have three or four ideas developing at once. **19** ☐ In the afternoon I try to focus on something in particular, such as a painting or sculpture.

I think it is very important to get things finished, so on the last Friday of every month I make a little exhibition for myself and even invite friends over to show what I have been doing. It keeps me motivated, knowing I have something to prepare for. **20** ☐

What advice would I give to other aspiring artists? Dedicate time to your art. Become part of a community. Social media is great, but it is also very important to have real-life meetings with other artists to share your ideas with.

Test 10

A   In the morning I am generally doing the preparation work for my ideas.

B   Even as a small child, I always enjoyed creating and making things.

C   Sometimes my friends even buy things, and that is an added incentive.

D   Art can be happy and sad, but overall I think art can be entertaining.

E   I would tell anyone who wants to be an artist to make sure that they keep producing things.

F   I've studied drawing, painting, jewellery making, and sculpture.

G   More than anything I've always enjoyed seeing the beauty around us, and noticing how art can make life more manageable and colourful.

H   Well, for me, becoming a professional artist was a decision I made later in life.

Part 5

Questions 21–26

For each question, choose the correct answer.

Google Inc.

If you **(21)**_____ the internet, you have probably used the Google search engine. More than 70% of all web searches worldwide happen on the Google platform.

Google Inc. was founded by Larry Page and Sergey Brin. The pair, **(22)**_____ had met at Stanford University, began working on a new type of search technology in 1996. Their objective was to list results by relevance, and how useful they could be to the user who is searching. They did this by finding out how **(23)**_____ links to other sites were found on a webpage, instead of just how many times the word appeared on the page.

Searches work differently nowadays. Google makes a huge amount of money, and 80% of that **(24)**_____ comes from Google's ads. Companies can pay to advertise their product and to appear higher in search results. With around 1.2 billion websites (estimated in 2022) in the world, it is no surprise that the whole process has **(25)**_____ more complicated.

Brin and Page established a corporate philosophy that included the phrases: 'Fast is better than slow'; 'You can make money without doing evil'; and 'Focus on the user and all else will follow'. The pair have done **(26)**_____ well as anyone could imagine and shaped the internet.

21	A	use	B	walk	C	put	D	ride
22	A	where	B	that	C	who	D	what
23	A	do	B	many	C	much	D	few
24	A	ingress	B	income	C	gain	D	winnings
25	A	came	B	come	C	became	D	become
26	A	as	B	too	C	more	D	less

Test 10

Part 6

Questions 27–32

For each question, write the correct answer.
Write **one** word for each gap.

Face Masks

During the Covid-19 global pandemic the wearing of face coverings became mandatory **(27)**_____ over the world. After initial doubts about its practicality, society almost completely accepted the need **(28)**_____ wear the mask, in one form or another.

There were the recommended options; the FFP2 and surgical mask. These may have been required to get on public transport or into public spaces, depending **(29)**_____ the country's policy. Some people decided to make their own too, using new and recycled pieces of material. All sorts of masks **(30)**_____ be seen: plain, elegant, colourful, funny.

Face masks were **(31)**_____ so common in many parts of the world before the pandemic. However, even though a lot of the restrictions which were in place because **(32)**_____ Covid-19 have been lifted, many people continue to choose to wear their mask.

Answers

Cambridge B1 Preliminary Reading

Test 1

Part 1
| 1 | B | 2 | A | 3 | B | 4 | A | 5 | C |

Part 2
| 6 | D | 7 | F | 8 | G | 9 | C | 10 | A |

Part 3
| 11 | A | 12 | B | 13 | B | 14 | C | 15 | D |

Part 4
| 16 | C | 17 | A | 18 | G | 19 | B | 20 | F |

Part 5
| 21 | B | 22 | A | 23 | D | 24 | A | 25 | D | 26 | C |

Part 6
| 27 | how | 28 | to / they | 29 | to | 30 | as | 31 | it | 32 | you |

Test 2

Part 1
| 1 | B | 2 | A | 3 | B | 4 | A | 5 | B |

Part 2
| 6 | F | 7 | A | 8 | G | 9 | D | 10 | B |

Part 3
| 11 | C | 12 | D | 13 | B | 14 | C | 15 | D |

Part 4
| 16 | E | 17 | F | 18 | B | 19 | D | 20 | H |

Answers

Part 5

| 21 | C | 22 | A | 23 | C | 24 | A | 25 | C | 26 | D |

Part 6

| 27 | is | 28 | as | 29 | and | 30 | have | 31 | it | 32 | can |

Test 3

Part 1

| 1 | B | 2 | A | 3 | A | 4 | A | 5 | C |

Part 2

| 6 | H | 7 | D | 8 | C | 9 | B | 10 | A |

Part 3

| 11 | B | 12 | C | 13 | B | 14 | C | 15 | C |

Part 4

| 16 | E | 17 | F | 18 | A | 19 | C | 20 | G |

Part 5

| 21 | D | 22 | B | 23 | A | 24 | A | 25 | B | 26 | C |

Part 6

| 27 | by | 28 | It | 29 | the | 30 | is | 31 | for | 32 | who / that |

Test 4

Part 1

| 1 | C | 2 | B | 3 | B | 4 | A | 5 | B |

Cambridge B1 Preliminary Reading

Part 2									
6	D	7	G	8	F	9	A	10	B

Part 3									
11	B	12	D	13	B	14	A	15	B

Part 4									
16	E	17	B	18	H	19	F	20	A

Part 5									
21	C	22	A	23	C	24	B	25	D	26	A

Part 6									
27	of	28	can	29	has	30	at	31	never	32	not

Test 5

Part 1									
1	B	2	C	3	A	4	B	5	A

Part 2									
6	C	7	A	8	B	9	H	10	E

Part 3									
11	D	12	A	13	D	14	B	15	B

Part 4									
16	D	17	H	18	C	19	A	20	G

Part 5									
21	A	22	B	23	D	24	A	25	B	26	B

Answers

Part 6										
27	of	28	an	29	is/will	30	under	31	from	32	can / should

Test 6

Part 1										
1	A	2	B	3	A	4	C	5	B

Part 2										
6	F	7	B	8	A	9	E	10	C

Part 3										
11	D	12	B	13	D	14	B	15	D

Part 4										
16	C	17	F	18	B	19	E	20	G

Part 5												
21	C	22	B	23	B	24	C	25	B	26	A

Part 6												
27	what	28	been	29	If	30	to	31	on	32	or

Test 7

Part 1										
1	C	2	A	3	B	4	A	5	A

Part 2										
6	D	7	E	8	F	9	B	10	A

Cambridge B1 Preliminary Reading

Part 3

| 11 | C | 12 | C | 13 | B | 14 | A | 15 | B |

Part 4

| 16 | H | 17 | B | 18 | E | 19 | F | 20 | A |

Part 5

| 21 | B | 22 | A | 23 | A | 24 | C | 25 | B | 26 | D |

Part 6

| 27 | has | 28 | and | 29 | at | 30 | your | 31 | the | 32 | an |

Test 8

Part 1

| 1 | B | 2 | A | 3 | A | 4 | B | 5 | C |

Part 2

| 6 | H | 7 | A | 8 | B | 9 | G | 10 | C |

Part 3

| 11 | C | 12 | B | 13 | D | 14 | C | 15 | A |

Part 4

| 16 | D | 17 | E | 18 | A | 19 | G | 20 | B |

Part 5

| 21 | C | 22 | A | 23 | C | 24 | B | 25 | B | 26 | A |

Part 6

| 27 | at | 28 | to | 29 | not | 30 | any | 31 | bring | 32 | is |

Answers

Test 9

Part 1
| 1 | B | 2 | C | 3 | B | 4 | A | 5 | C |

Part 2
| 6 | H | 7 | D | 8 | A | 9 | G | 10 | B |

Part 3
| 11 | C | 12 | C | 13 | C | 14 | A | 15 | B |

Part 4
| 16 | C | 17 | A | 18 | F | 19 | H | 20 | E |

Part 5
| 21 | B | 22 | C | 23 | C | 24 | A | 25 | B | 26 | A |

Part 6
| 27 | in | 28 | to | 29 | for | 30 | and | 31 | up | 32 | because |

Test 10

Part 1
| 1 | A | 2 | C | 3 | B | 4 | A | 5 | C |

Part 2
| 6 | F | 7 | A | 8 | C | 9 | E | 10 | B |

Part 3
| 11 | C | 12 | B | 13 | A | 14 | C | 15 | C |

Part 4
| 16 | H | 17 | B | 18 | F | 19 | A | 20 | C |

Cambridge B1 Preliminary Reading

Part 5

| 21 | A | 22 | C | 23 | B | 24 | B | 25 | D | 26 | A |

Part 6

| 27 | all | 28 | to | 29 | on | 30 | could | 31 | not | 32 | of |

www.ingramcontent.com/pod-product-compliance
Lightning Source LLC
Chambersburg PA
CBHW050717090526
44588CB00014B/2319